MOTHER TROUBLE

Mediations of White Maternal Angst after Second
Wave Feminism

MOTHER TROUBLE

Mediations of White Maternal
Angst after Second
Wave Feminism

Miranda J. Brady

UNIVERSITY OF TORONTO PRESS
Toronto Buffalo London

ISBN 978-1-4875-5693-8 (cloth)   ISBN 978-1-4875-5695-2 (EPUB)
ISBN 978-1-4875-5694-5 (PDF)

Library and Archives Canada Cataloguing in Publication
Title: Mother trouble : mediations of white maternal angst after
   second wave feminism / Miranda J. Brady.
Names: Brady, Miranda J., author.
Description: Includes bibliographical references and index.
Identifiers: Canadiana (print) 20240408772 | Canadiana (ebook)
   20240408799 | ISBN 9781487556938 (cloth) |
   ISBN 9781487556945 (PDF) | ISBN 9781487556952 (EPUB)
Subjects: LCSH: Motherhood in popular culture. | LCSH: Mothers –
   Social conditions. | LCSH: Women, White – Social conditions. |
   LCSH: Second-wave feminism.
Classification: LCC HQ759 .B727 2024 | DDC 306.874/3–dc23

Cover design: Val Cooke
Cover image: *Mother's Day*/Claudia Sauter (Poptonicart)/Artmajeur

We wish to acknowledge the land on which the University of Toronto
Press operates. This land is the traditional territory of the Wendat, the
Anishnaabeg, the Haudenosaunee, the Métis, and the Mississaugas of the
Credit First Nation.

This book has been published with the help of a grant from the
Federation for the Humanities and Social Sciences, through the Awards
to Scholarly Publications Program, using funds provided by the Social
Sciences and Humanities Research Council of Canada.

University of Toronto Press acknowledges the financial support of the
Government of Canada, the Canada Council for the Arts, and the Ontario
Arts Council, an agency of the Government of Ontario, for its publishing
activities.

Canada Council   Conseil des Arts
for the Arts   du Canada

ONTARIO ARTS COUNCIL
CONSEIL DES ARTS DE L'ONTARIO
an Ontario government agency
un organisme du gouvernement de l'Ontario

Funded by the   Financé par le
Government   gouvernement
of Canada   du Canada

Canada

This book is dedicated to mothers.

Contents

Acknowledgments

No author is an island, and that was certainly true with respect to this book. There are so many people who contributed in various ways. First, I'd like to thank Sandy Russill for her emotional support and many hours of childcare, both of which enabled me to write this book. I would also like to thank friends, colleagues, and students who patiently provided feedback as I developed my ideas, including Chris Russill, Shoshana Magnet, Jackie Kennelly and the Cozy Mamas Writing Group, Sheryl Hamilton, Neil Gerlach, Sarah Brouillette, Dylan Frietag, Melodie Cardin, Emily Hiltz, and Erika Christiansen. Josh Greenberg and all my colleagues and students in Carleton University's Communication and Media Studies program were extremely supportive and helpful, as were those in the Canadian Communication Association, where I presented early versions of three chapters. I would also like to thank Carleton's Faculty of Public Affairs for providing research and travel support so that I could share and develop the book with other scholars nationally and internationally. My research assistant, Jenny Kliever, was especially patient and helpful with production issues as the manuscript neared completion. I will forever be thankful to other friends and colleagues who have shaped my thinking over the years: Matt McAllister, Jeremy Packer, Salma Monani, John M.H. Kelly, and Sarah Sharma, just to name a few. I owe a huge debt of gratitude to two brilliant peer reviewers who provided thoughtful feedback to help strengthen the manuscript, and those who provided feedback on earlier iterations of chapters

2 and 4, which were published in *Feminist Media Studies* and the *Journal of Gender Studies*, respectively. I'd also like to thank my editor, Mark Thompson, and the University of Toronto Press editorial board for believing in the book. Finally, thank you to my partner and kids, and a special acknowledgment of my mother for all her time and energy in caring for me. Of all her influences, her incredible work ethic and love of horror are two of my favourite.

Acknowledgments

No author is an island, and that was certainly true with respect to this book. There are so many people who contributed in various ways. First, I'd like to thank Sandy Russill for her emotional support and many hours of childcare, both of which enabled me to write this book. I would also like to thank friends, colleagues, and students who patiently provided feedback as I developed my ideas, including Chris Russill, Shoshana Magnet, Jackie Kennelly and the Cozy Mamas Writing Group, Sheryl Hamilton, Neil Gerlach, Sarah Brouillette, Dylan Frietag, Melodie Cardin, Emily Hiltz, and Erika Christiansen. Josh Greenberg and all my colleagues and students in Carleton University's Communication and Media Studies program were extremely supportive and helpful, as were those in the Canadian Communication Association, where I presented early versions of three chapters. I would also like to thank Carleton's Faculty of Public Affairs for providing research and travel support so that I could share and develop the book with other scholars nationally and internationally. My research assistant, Jenny Kliever, was especially patient and helpful with production issues as the manuscript neared completion. I will forever be thankful to other friends and colleagues who have shaped my thinking over the years: Matt McAllister, Jeremy Packer, Salma Monani, John M.H. Kelly, and Sarah Sharma, just to name a few. I owe a huge debt of gratitude to two brilliant peer reviewers who provided thoughtful feedback to help strengthen the manuscript, and those who provided feedback on earlier iterations of chapters

2 and 4, which were published in *Feminist Media Studies* and the *Journal of Gender Studies*, respectively. I'd also like to thank my editor, Mark Thompson, and the University of Toronto Press editorial board for believing in the book. Finally, thank you to my partner and kids, and a special acknowledgment of my mother for all her time and energy in caring for me. Of all her influences, her incredible work ethic and love of horror are two of my favourite.

MOTHER TROUBLE

chapter one

Unfinished Business

In the 1975 film *The Stepford Wives*, an association of white, suburban men conspire to replace the wives and mothers of their town with robots who delight in domestic labour and serve them without question. The pleasant android homemakers of Stepford could be considered the perverse doppelgangers of real feminist activists of that era, including those of the international Wages for Housework movement (Federici and Austin 2017; Toupin 2018). Unlike the wives of Stepford, these second wave feminists demanded acknowledgment and compensation for the copious amounts of invisible and unwaged labour performed by women globally, which included the work of mothering (Federici and Austin 2017; James 2012).[1] Fifty years later, many people still remember the archetype of the Stepford wife, but most have forgotten about Wages for Housework.

Despite apparent gains in paid labour for women since second wave feminism, those engaged in the work of mothering still continue to perform grossly disproportionate amounts of unpaid labour, which affects them financially, professionally, and emotionally (Moyser and Burlock 2018; Barroso and Horowitz 2021; Watson 2020; O'Reilly 2020). Overall, women in Canada still assume a heavier work burden than men, when both waged and unwaged work are taken into account (Moyser and Burlock 2018). The United States lags far behind so-called developed nations in ensuring paid parental and sick leave, which might better enable mothers to participate in paid labour (Livingston & Thomas 2019;

Hawkins 2020); this, despite the fact that, in 2019, in almost half the households with two parents, both parents worked full time (Livingston and Thomas 2019). Many mothers in the United States, particularly Hispanic, Black, and Asian workers, cannot access or afford to take maternity leave (Hawkins 2020).

While improving, the gender pay gap for mothers – the "motherhood penalty" – is still especially pronounced (Bjornholt 2020, 393).[2] Moreover, the inaccessibility and high cost of childcare often make paid work outside the home untenable for mothers (Institute for Gender and the Economy 2022). Amidst these desperate conditions, a precarious and underpaid class of workers largely comprising immigrants and women of colour provides domestic labour for middle-class families (Cheah 2007; Duffy 2007; Gilligan 1982; Henaway 2023). We can situate the phenomenon of gendered migrant and racialized domestic work as part of a longer legacy of racialized gendered labour exploitation (Davis 1981; Collins 1990), which assumes new forms under current economic conditions (Henaway 2023).

Many mothers lack the very basics of survival for themselves and their children. Even prior to the COVID-19 pandemic, mothers raising children under eighteen years represented 50–60 per cent of homeless women in the United States (David, Gelberg and Suchman 2012); lone mothers in London, England, were eight times more likely than couples with children to experience homelessness (BBC, 2018), which is closely linked to social determinants of health like shorter life expectancy, depression, and mental health struggles (Strafford and Wood 2017). With the 2022 US Supreme Court's decision to overturn *Roe v. Wade*, the retraction of reproductive rights so hard won in the second wave will inevitably perpetuate the poverty under which mothers and children disproportionately suffer, as choices in reproductive planning are foreclosed (Stolberg 2020; Totenberg and McCammon 2022).

Unequal social impacts experienced by mothers are intensified for those of a lower socio-economic status and minoritized groups. This is especially the case in times of crisis, as has been apparent during the global pandemic (Thomas, Henderson, and Horton 2022). For example, Black populations in the United States experienced higher rates of death from COVID-19 (Ray 2020; Friedman and Satterthwaite 2021). Regardless of their class, Black mothers already faced health disparities, such as higher maternal mortality rates (Louisias and Marrast 2020) and higher rates of infant mortality and birth complications, all of which are "indicative of systemic racism" (Harrell 2021, 331).

Over the past several decades, feminists have fought for reasonable supports that would greatly benefit all mothers, including services that would more evenly distribute the burdens of domestic labour (Toupin 2018); access to affordable childcare, housing, and healthcare (Davis 1981; Romney 2021; Campbell, Dawson and Gidney 2022); pay equity and workplace justice (Cobble 2004); and a universal family allowance (Toupin 2018) and standard basic income (Bjornholt 2020; McKay 2001).[3] This fight extended through the 1960s and 1970s with various strands of the second wave (Echols 2002).

While feminist strategies are often associated with the National Organization for Women (NOW), lesser-known second wave collectives, including socialist, Black, and Third World women's movements, had their own aims (Davis 1981; Romney 2021; Combahee River Collective [1977] 2017; Taylor 2017). One key shortcoming of mainstream white-led movements like NOW was their focus on gender and their corresponding failure to recognize other systems of oppression that affected entire communities in which women (and mothers) were interconnected (Romney 2021; Echols 2002; Taylor 2017).

Other groups paid more mind to these intersections; these included the Third World Women's Alliance, which was an international movement including women of colour, women in the Global South, and Indigenous women (Romney 2021; Boyer 1997; Third World Woman's Alliance [1971] 2016). The Combahee River Collective, a Black- and lesbian-led socialist feminist group, addressed similar concerns. Black and Third World feminists offered nuanced arguments around gender equity to illustrate the ways in which race, class, imperialism, and homophobia also played an "interlocking" role in social oppression within capitalism (Combahee River Collective, [1977] 2017, 260). As they argued, this complex system exacerbated hardships experienced by all their relations, which were marked by racism, police brutality, incarceration, dispossession, environmental exploitation, and impoverishment (Combahee River Collective [1977] 2017; Romney 2021; Moreton-Robinson [2000] 2020; Boyer 1997; Davis 1981; Collins 1994; Story 2014; Taylor 2017). The problems faced by mothers in these communities could be remedied only by addressing the underlying conditions. As Patricia Hill Collins notes, "For women of color, the subjective experience of mothering/motherhood is inextricably linked to the sociocultural concerns of racial ethnic communities – one does not exist without the other" (1994, 372).

The same struggles persist today, even as feminists debate the characteristics of our current feminist epoch and whether it is substantially different from former feminist eras (Rivers 2017; Campbell, Dawson, and Gidney 2022). Yet, while second wave movements like Wages for Housework pointed out the problems capitalism posed for mothers, including the valorization of individualized wage earners at the expense of those who perform unwaged care (James [1975] 2012), neoliberalism has only intensified these conditions (Vandenbeld Giles 2014a). While second wave feminists argued for the socialization of childcare and welfare supports, many of these services have been commodified and privatized, leading to untenable costs (Bjornholt 2020). This has also been the case for various aspects of healthcare, leading many to take their health and that of their children into their own hands (S. King 2008; Jack 2014). While feminist economists point out the ways in which a universal basic income could reduce poverty as well as help mitigate the costs of unpaid reproductive labour (McKay 2001; Cantillon and McLean 2016), red baiting and conservative welfare reform have made it difficult to advance socialized services in the United States (Briggs 2018).

These are just some of the ways in which the possibilities of second wave feminism have failed to materialize for mothers. Though not always acknowledged as such, these missed opportunities continue to manifest in our popular imaginary, but mostly with reference to the struggles of white, cisgender women. As this book argues, the discourse of angst around white motherhood in popular media reflects the unrealized potential and omissions of the second wave as we inhabit a newer feminist era.[4]

While many strains of second wave feminism offered alternative futures that would benefit all mothers, the goals of mainstream feminism to achieve gender equity in paid work overshadowed other possibilities and sidelined reproductive labour (Toupin 2018), treating it as a retrograde afterthought. This narrow strategy, combined with conservative backlash in the 1980s, curtailed variations on the second wave that more fully addressed interlocking systems of oppression (Taylor 2017). It also foreclosed critiques of the broader capitalist system that acknowledged reproductive labour *as* labour (Federici 2014; James 2012), thereby missing an opportunity to validate the work performed by mothers and, by extension, to validate mothers themselves. These erasures, combined with the persistence of mother blame, as part and parcel of a devaluation of motherwork, continue to cause problems for all mothers. The troubles of white mothers, who are hyper-visible in popular media, are just one symptom of much deeper inequities that continue to haunt all mothers after second wave feminism.

For example, the "juggling mother," a white woman who performs an acceptable level of "coming undone" in balancing her professional work and homelife, is a common trope in contemporary popular media (Watson 2020, 25). She is depicted in the CBC show *Workin' Moms* and similar popular cultural texts like the 2011 film *I Don't Know How She Does It*. In these depictions, white mothers are seen bending to the unreasonable, neoliberal demands of professional and family life (Watson 2020). When they do protest, this is portrayed as a personal choice rather than a challenge to the underlying economic conditions that enable their exploitation, and there is no serious repercussion to their economic or professional status – in fact, they are rewarded for asserting themselves. In the 2018 film *Tully*, Marlo (played by actress Charlize Theron), the mother of three young children, experiences an overwhelming lack of support and a (postpartum) crisis that leads her to a psychotic break. However, like the aforementioned media depictions, personal transformation takes place, but no overarching, lasting, or systemic solution is offered. In providing a brief history leading up to mediations of white mothers like these (and reading against the grain to think about the racialized mothers we do not see), this book contextualizes them as a continuation of the trouble of motherhood, which was never resolved during the second wave.

If motherhood is feminism's "unfinished business" (O'Reilly 2020, 51), how does this tension play out in our popular imaginary? More specifically, since white motherhood is overrepresented in popular media and has historically been constructed as the prototypical ideal of good motherhood (Collins 1994; Feldstein 2000), what does it mean that, since second wave feminism, white mothers have often been depicted as unsettled and dissatisfied in US and Canadian popular media? If Black motherhood has been constituted through controlling and reductive figures since the time of slavery (Collins 1990) and has also been employed to bolster ideals of good white liberal citizenship in modernity (Feldstein 2000), how has the figure of the white mother been reconfigured with social anxieties related to crisis and change over the past sixty years?[5]

As Andrea O'Reilly (2020, 2021) has argued, the goals of feminism and mothering need not be at odds, but rather, a "matricentric feminism" would recognize the specific challenges and work performed by mothers while avoiding the gender determinism that is often associated with the ideology of motherhood and maternalism. As this book argues, such a feminism would also address the devaluation of mothers and their unpaid work as well as the erasure of motherwork performed by women of colour and other minoritized groups in mediations of motherhood. This book explores long patterns of systemic injustice that are oppressive for mothers and that lead to their struggles. By contrast, popular media more often depict mothers themselves as the trouble.

A Hundred Years of Mother Trouble

Previous research has detailed anxiety around motherhood over more than a century, exploring the ways in which it has been problematized, mobilized, weaponized, and, even when valorized, accompanied by an unsavory, Janus-faced other (Ehrenreich and

English 1978; Plant 2010). For example, scholarship has explored shifts from Victorian notions of moral maternalism, where (white) mothers were seen as moral guardians for their families and society more broadly, to the emergence of Freudian-influenced scientific mothering and critiques around overbearing "momism" (Ehrenreich and English 1978; Plant 2010, 2, 24). It has illustrated modern ideas of mother blame (Caplan 2010) in the interwar and mid-century periods, during which mothers were singled out as the key obstacles to their children's development and that of society, either because, apparently, they selfishly smothered or were too cold to their children (Ehrenreich and English 1978; Ladd-Taylor and Umansky 1998). As an extension of these ideas, and due to deeply entrenched ableism, misogyny, and a lack of systemic supports, mother blame continues today for mothers of disabled and neurodivergent children (Blum 2007; Douglas and Klar 2020), who will not be moulded into the capitalist model of the ideal and independent producer/consumer (Fritsch 2015; McGuire 2016). This ableist pressure towards conformity is one example of the ways in which discourses of motherhood are used to reproduce and naturalize the economic status quo.

The good mother/bad mother binary has been deployed for centuries. "Good mothers" (the ultimate symbol of which is the Virgin Mary) are depicted as self-sacrificing and nurturing at all costs (Ladd-Taylor and Umansky 1998; Caplan 2010; Ehrenreich and English 1978). "Bad mothers," by contrast, are often coded by race and class, and are pointed to as a convenient scapegoat for broader social problems like poverty and to illustrate proper forms of white civic engagement and population health (Feldstein 2000; Ehrenreich and English 1978).[6] Notable racialized bad mother archetypes have included the 1980s Black welfare queen, who gamed the system of social benefits, and the matriarch, who emasculated Black men by assuming the role of domineering, single head of the household (Collins 1990).

White trash mother archtypes have also been employed in poverty-shaming discourses that attribute lower socio-economic status to mothers themselves, despite the overwhelming odds against upward mobility that they face (Dobson, and Knezevic

2017). McRobbie describes the "subdued moral panic" around young white working-class mothers in the 1980s and 1990s and their apparent "dependency culture" (2000 159, 175). According to conservative discourse of that era, such mothers opted out of the job market in favour of having babies and a reliance on state welfare. By contrast, McRobbie relays their broader social struggles, including joblessness among their partners, a lack of apprenticeships and upward mobility in pink-collar labour, and loss of welfare benefits for mothers when entering employment, even when only part-time. However, as with the welfare queen, the archetype of the "undeserving" young, white welfare mother persists in popular media (McRobbie 2020, 99). Each of these figures has been a tool in conservative strategies to undermine liberal programs of social welfare and to deny the actual systems of economic oppression in which many mothers struggle (Briggs 2018; McRobbie 2020).

Key works have also identified newer pressures associated with (mostly white professional class) motherhood after the second wave, such as intensive mothering, exemplified by a high-performance career women who is also responsible for the moral, intellectual, spiritual, and emotional development of her children, inevitably leading to a sense of inadequacy (Hays 1998). Others have traced the phenomenon of post-feminist "mompreneurs" adapting to the demands of late modern capitalism to fold their paid and domestic labour together (Briggs 2018; Vandenbeld Giles 2014a; Anderson and Moore 2014; Watson 2020).[7] Still others have critiqued celebrity culture's wellness and fitness influences, now adding bodywork to the regime of impossible aesthetic lifestyle demands for mothers (O'Brien Hallstein 2016). Finally, recent work has identified the discourse of "mothers behaving badly," or white mothers temporarily acting out in response to the unrealized goals of gender equity and pressures of career-life balance in films like Bad Moms, but resulting in no real systemic reforms (Littler 2020, 499).

Taken together, all of this scholarship paints a picture of unease underpinning white motherhood, which is never good enough, but over-represented in popular culture. At the same time, the hyper-focus on white mothers in popular media has largely meant the omission of mothering by racial and ethnic minorities. In discussing feminist understandings of mediation, Sarah Sharma reminds us that "sexism and racism are always tied to the technological," and it is the role of media studies scholars to uncover the ways in which media help to maintain power inequities (2022, 9). If media are extensions of "man," as Marshall McLuhan ([1964] 2001) posited, then they are also an extension of his cultural values. In thinking about the shape and form motherhood assumes and the ubiquity of whiteness in popular culture, we can also understand the role of mediated maternal bodies as they work to "produce race" (Sharma 2022, 9) and prototypical motherhood, adding more layers to the existing oppressions of motherhood as a patriarchal institution (Rich 1976). While economic pressures, gender inequity, and misogyny are still barriers faced by all mothers, the orientation (Ahmed 2010) and corporality of white maternal bodies has meant higher degrees of social access and privilege as they help to define what motherhood means through their hyper-visibility.[8]

Anxieties of Whiteness

Whiteness is more than a biological construct, aesthetic, or phenotype; it is historically contingent and varies based on geography and culture (Dyer 2017). It is also a ubiquitous sensibility accompanied by a sense of entitlement and is often overlooked as a racial category at all, making white privilege seem natural (Zakaria 2021; Dyer 2005, 2017). Historically, the commodification and mediation of Black and brown bodies has helped to ensure and naturalize white privilege (Towns 2022), which is deeply and psychically entrenched (Fanon [1952] 2008).

Though insidious and persistent historically, tensions over racism came to a head with the 2020 death of George Floyd, a Black Minneapolis man, at the hands of a white police officer, which was filmed and circulated widely. Tensions over racial inequity have flared up through media events of the past, like the 1992 Los Angeles riots following the acquittal of police officers filmed beating Rodney King. However, Floyd's death and the #BlackLivesMatter movement, which predated but amplified this tragedy, called into question white privilege as a "default norm" in unprecedented ways (Dubrofsky 2022, 11).

For some white mothers, challenges to white privilege may involve a sense of discomfort. Some may feel that they have been decentred, as attention has turned to forms of inequity such as the legacies of racism and colonization (Zakaria 2021; Major 2021; National Inquiry 2019; Taylor 2016). As with masculinity crises that have been evoked by feminist movements since the nineteenth century (Gee and Jackson 2017), some white mothers may attribute their own struggles to social movements by marginalized groups since the civil rights era. DiAngelo (2018) might describe this defensive feeling of victimhood as "white fragility." Carole Anderson (2016) described similar feelings of resentment in seeing Black bodies as a threat to white advantage as "white rage." While the rage Anderson notes may be nefariously manifested and covert (e.g., decisions around redlining made from the safety of boardrooms), more unabashed strains continue to exist.

Over the past several decades, conservative lobbying has exploited white maternal struggle and anxiety. A right-wing movement of white women, first emerging in response to second wave feminism (Tillson 1996), has embraced traditional gender roles, rejected feminism, and employed a kind of "reasonable racism" (Armour 1997), where people of colour are simply avoided through homeschooling, charter schools, and siloed, homogenized communities. In more recent years, this sentiment has been naturalized through conservative social media influencers. For example, Darby (2020) argues that white motherhood is weaponized by white supremacists identifying with extremist groups through the aesthetically pleasing and blissful images of white family life that they post on social media. While such posts are often subtly racist, more outrageous calls for alt-right women to take up the "white baby challenge" speak to a conspiratorial fear of the "great replacement" theory, interpellating white women to employ their uteruses as good white (nationalist) citizens (Darby 2020; Stern 2019).

Christian white motherhood has also been used as a tool to claw back reproductive rights and social welfare (Darby 2020; Briggs 2018), in keeping with the tradition of mobilizing motherhood for political purposes. However, while it is easy to critique the racist and defensive treatments of right-wing motherhood, the valorization of white motherhood in ways that disadvantage minoritized groups is a strategy that comes from both the left and right (Plant, 2010; Feldstein, 2000). As these strategies are continuously shifting with political tides, the stakes in employing motherhood as a critical analytic are as important as ever.

Mother Trouble as Epistemology

The title *Mother Trouble* refers not only to mothers as feminism's "unfinished business" (O'Reilly 2020), but also to the theoretical and epistemological trouble motherhood opens up. It employs a feminist critical/cultural framework that takes social realms as well as structural inequality seriously. The book combines feminist Foucauldian thinking around discourse with Marxist, anticolonial, and critical race theory to study culture as an "arena of social production" and therefore as "one area of feminist struggle" (Hennessy and Ingraham 1997). The approach in this book follows a healthy tradition of transdisciplinary cultural studies, which strikes a balance by both employing, and turning a critical lens on, the basic assumptions of Marxist and Foucauldian thought (see, e.g., Hall 1997; Browne 2015; Couthard 2014).

While gender is one important consideration, *Mother Trouble* invites us to think about the trouble of a singular and restricted focus as we challenge systems of power in motherhood. The title of this book is a nod to Judith Butler's (1990) seminal proclamation that gender is discursive and performative. Similarly, motherhood as a discursive regime and practice, constitutes and interpellates women (O'Reilly 2020). Underlying both Butler's *Gender Trouble* and this book is an understanding of discourse as a system of knowledge reproduced across cultural sites, which makes some possibilities available while delimiting or foreclosing others (Foucault 1977); it is also important to understand the ways in which inequitable relations of power are maintained and reproduced through discourse (Foucault 1980), and the ways in which the subject and the body are constituted (or gain meaning) through discursive formations (Foucault 1977; 1982). Motherhood as a discursive regime is a highly gendered patriarchal institution in which particular performances and rituals are internalized and expected (Rich 1976). However, in contrast to motherhood, the norms and practices of mothering and motherwork vary dramatically in different economic, racial, and socio-cultural contexts (Collins 1994; Story 2014).

In thinking beyond discursive regimes, structural failures make mothers and children the most impoverished people in the world and force them to contort around unreasonable neoliberal conditions (Vandenbeld Giles 2014b). Marxist theory provides some tools that allow us to interrogate motherhood within the structures of capitalism, but many theorists, such as Hennessy and Ingraham (1997) and Vogel ([1983] 2013), have grappled with the theoretical troubles of combining Marxism with feminism. In short, Marx left a foundation inadequate for addressing problems of inequity beyond those of class – for example, gender, race, and colonization (Couthard 2014). While Marx ([1867] 1977) argued that women should be kept outside of industrialized labour and therefore capitalism, Engels ([1884] 2016) contended that women's integration into the workplace would help to flatten gender inequality (Barrett and McIntosh 1982). However, both theorists fell short in their analysis of gender. As discussed further in chapter 2, socialist feminists such as Silvia Federici (2014, 2020) extended the ideas of Marx and Engels to argue that capitalism erected divisions between genders by encouraging a particular exploitation of women due to their ability to reproduce labour power. Though Marx did not consider domestic labour to be actual labour in the capitalist sense, as it produced only use value rather than surplus value and commodities, Federici, James (2012), Dalla Costa ([1972] 2016), and other socialist feminists recognized the role of mothers in social reproduction, and the divisions erected through wage relations in which women were subordinated.

Conversely, as Toupin (2018) points out, mainstream, white-led, second wave feminists tended not to draw attention to unwaged reproductive labour, as they believed that this was a retrograde strategy that would distract from gender equity in paid labour and alternatives for women outside the confines of the family. Rather, they encouraged greater task-sharing between parents and socialization of domestic labour.[9] However, given the statistics mentioned in the opening of this chapter, this approach was flawed and, I would argue, a denial of the actual work that is performed and necessary. The division in opinion over strategy (and fear that the wrong strategy would derail feminist goals), along with conservative backlash against the welfare state (Toupin 2018), meant that the issue of unpaid and underpaid gendered labour would not be resolved, with compounding effects that continue today for all mothers. In reflecting on the persistence of unequal labour performed by mothers in the twenty-first century, I would argue that the focus on workplace equality and task-sharing did not account for the underlying factors that would make both impossible, including the relations of power reproduced by privileging the ideal and individualistic wage-earner. This focus also did not account for the undervalued work and care necessary to sustain life.

This wage relation also disadvantaged people of colour, who experienced racism in seeking paid work and who often performed devalued forms of labour (Barbara Smith, cited in Taylor 2017), including reproductive labour, in many cases for white families (Collins 1990; Davis 1981). In other words, while gender is one important consideration in the study of motherhood, an interrogation of the troubles that mothers face must also centre wage relations, economic structure, and race, as a set of interlocking concerns.

In considering these tensions, this book takes as its point of departure second wave feminism and its associated "shaky ground" (Echols 2002). It traces the angst that already existed in relation to white feminism and motherhood with a main source of tension around abundant forms of inequity (Moreton-Robinson [2000] 2020; Zakaria 2021; hooks [1981] 2015). Though the focus of this book is not affect theory it attempts – along with other related studies in motherhood (Watson 2020), feminism (Ahmed 2017; Campbell, Dawson and Gidney 2022), and whiteness (Dubrofsky 2022) – to understand maternal angst as a discourse with implications for a felt reality that is both instigated and conscripted through media.

The feeling of white maternal angst could be described as a sense of being exploited, profoundly under-supported, overworked, judged, and misunderstood, with the fear that economic and social precarity are always at the gate.

For the purposes of this book, reproductive labour can be understood as the work of sustaining life; it includes, "various kinds of work- mental, manual, and emotional- aimed at providing the historically and socially, as well as biologically, defined care necessary to maintain existing life and to reproduce the next generation" (Laslett and Brenner 1989, 383); it includes both paid and unpaid forms (Davis 1981; Duffy 2007; Collins 1990).

This book assumes that motherwork extends beyond essentialized gender roles "to anyone who does the work of mothering as a central part of her or his life" (O'Reilly 2020, 51). It also acknowledges the importance of non-biological "other-mothering" and systems of support in Black and racialized communities, while noting the systemic racism that necessitates them (Story 2014; Collins 1994). Unfortunately, these more enlarged views of mothering are scarcely reflected in the popular cultural terrain. Thus, the examples in this book, with some exceptions, focus mostly on white cisgender women as biological mother figures who have a virtual monopoly in popular media, allowing us to turn a critical eye on pervasive discursive assumptions about motherhood.

Orienting the Chapters and Analysis

Through selected examples in popular films, novels, memes, and television shows, each chapter of this book narrows in on popular media in order to think about white maternal angst as a manifestation of second wave feminism's unrealized possibilities and continued omissions. Examples explore English-language media from the United States and Canada, and they illustrate the ways in which the discourse of white maternal angst transcends various media texts, shapes, forms, and genres.

Starting with the novels and filmic adaptations of *Rosemary's Baby* and *The Stepford Wives*, chapter 2 asks how the struggles of second wave feminism manifested in unsettling depictions and omissions of reproductive labour in the 1960s and 1970s.[10] Chapter 3 critically engages neoliberal motherhood in home renovation reality television, demonstrating how late-modern capitalism, post-feminist discourse, and global media flows encourage (mostly white homeowner) mothers to internalize an exploitative system of wealth accumulation in which only the privileged benefit. Chapter 4 takes the millennial turn as its point of departure, examining memes on Reddit to explore the emergence of anti-vaxx moms and Karen figures in popular understandings of white privilege, mother blame, ableism, and distrust of health authorities. Chapter 5 employs analysis of white maternal estrangement and mother blame in the television shows *Modern Family* and *Shameless* to illustrate the televisual techniques used to punish mothers who opt out of proper reproductive labour. Finally, through an analysis of HBO's dystopic science fiction show *Raised by Wolves*, chapter 6 explores a future of continuing angst for an ageing, maternal, "white saviour" android amidst environmental catastrophe.

While an overarching theoretical and epistemological framework centred on critical and cultural feminism guides this book, unique bodies of research and methods are called upon as needed to engage with specific content. In *Media, Society, World*, Nick Couldry identifies the "four apexes" of media theory and analysis: textual/content analysis to explore the ideological underpinnings of a media text; political economy, which involves studies in production, distribution, and audience reception; medium theory, exploring the "technical properties" of media; and social uses, which, he explains, require theorization around the "social process that media constitute and enable" (2012 8, 6). Though the main focus of this book relates to the analysis of media content and its relationship with social processes, it employs each of the approaches noted by Couldry.

Each chapter involves a creative and historically informed feminist Foucauldian discourse analysis to trace white maternal angst across various media sites. Chapter 4 also develops a visual discourse analysis to examine still images and to contextualize and historicize their circulation online through Web 2.0. While there was little space to explore audience reception, this chapter also provides a sense of audience/participant sentiment by examining the dialectic of "good" and "bad" mothers in memes. Similarly, chapter 3 employs political economy techniques to trace the funding, cultural policies, and global flows that enable transmediated discourses of neoliberal motherhood in HGTV shows. In addition to exploring content, chapter 5 seeks to understand how the "technical properties" or form (R. Williams 1974) and techniques of television shows shape and guide audience reception of absent mothers, keeping in mind that reception varies by subject position (Hall [1973] 1991).

The analysis in this book asks us to identify not only what is there, but what has been omitted. If these media texts are about white motherhood, what is the subtext when we read them creatively and against the grain (Said 1993)? Analysis in the book has inevitably strayed from the creators' intent. For example, it is doubtful that sci-fi director Ridley Scott had menopausal transition in mind when he created *Raised by Wolves*. As with all chapters, the analysis provided does not assume a detached objectivity, but I do hope it guides readers to ask important questions about real phenomena. A more holistic approach might have examined media in different languages or a plethora of other available examples, but, alas, the author and book were limited in scope and talents.

In the spirit of situating the author's own subject position, I am a cisgender woman living on unceded, unsurrendered Algonquin territories and recognize my privilege in being white and having access to waged labour. In addition to my full-time employment, I spend anywhere from four to ten hours on most days performing unwaged reproductive labour, which can be physically and emotionally taxing. I am the mother of two children, one of whom requires an intensive amount of care.[11] The profound lack of support following the birth of my second child is what led me to the study of motherhood and a critique of the current conditions in which it takes place.

A note about chapter 4: unlike the other solo-authored chapters in this book, this chapter was co-authored with Emily Hiltz and Erika Christiansen. Although a bit of a deviation, this chapter makes an important contribution to motherhood studies and media studies as it demonstrates representations of the "bad mother" across digital and participatory media platforms. While we often value single authorship (as with individualized wage earners), I am lucky to be situated in a nourishing intellectual community, including students and colleagues who first introduced me to "Karen" several years ago, before that figure became so prolific; I owe them a debt of gratitude.

chapter two

"I Think the Men Are Behind It": Reproductive Labour and the Horror of Second Wave Feminism

"They say it is love. We say it is unwaged work."

(Federici (1975) 2020b, 11)

From the late 1960s through the mid-1970s, women in horror films had a lot on their plates.[1] When their children weren't possessed by demons, they were grappling with sexual harassment and satanic cults. Films like *Rosemary's Baby* (1968) and *The Stepford Wives* (1975), based on popular novels by Ira Levin, highlighted persistent and competing anxieties emerging with second wave feminism about what it meant to be liberated. The struggles playing out in these films reflected the anxieties of a tumultuous historical period. It is no coincidence that protagonists like Rosemary Woodhouse (*Rosemary's Baby*) and Joanna Eberhart (*The Stepford Wives*) emerged on the brink of the women's liberation movement and the formation of different strands of radical, socialist, and Black feminisms. The struggles against the tethers of patriarchy and "domestic slavery" point to central concerns of feminists at that time (Davis 1981, 303).

Many scholars have written about women, horror and the patriarchal, and panoptic regulation of the abject female body, mostly employing a psychoanalytic framework (e.g., Arnold 2013; Clover 1992; Creed 1992; Kristeva 1982; Ussher 2006). Male anxieties over the monstrous female have appeared throughout history in such figures as the Greco-Roman Medusa and the vagina dentata (Ussher 2006), the monstrous woman (and womb), the witch, the vampire, the possessed/hysterical woman (Creed 1992), and the monstrous, archaic mother (Arnold 2013; Creed 1992; Harrington 2018; Kristeva 1982; Short 2007). Despite the abundance of literature about horror and gender, surprisingly little has focused on horror and reproductive labour, which is an oversight, given the concerns of feminist groups in the late 1960s to 1970s and the centrality of domestic labour in popular novels and filmic horror adaptations like *The Stepford Wives*.

However, while such novels and films have been heralded as "feminist" due to their inclusion of feminist themes, they reflected the perspectives of their white male authors, directors, and intended audiences (Foertsch 2019, 102). Therefore, their treatment of feminism missed some important points of critique. Moreover, these stories centred on middle- and upper-class white women, paralleling the omissions of second wave feminism; they similarly marginalized the experiences of people of colour, who disproportionately performed low-wage reproductive labour for white people (Davis 1981; Taylor 2017; Combahee River Collective [1977] 2017).

As noted in the introduction, reproductive labour can be understood as "various kinds of work – mental, manual, and emotional – aimed at providing the historically and socially, as well as biologically, defined care necessary to maintain existing life and to reproduce the next generation" (Laslett and Brenner 1989, 383). It comprises both paid and unpaid forms (Davis 1981; Duffy 2007; Collins 1990). Examples of reproductive labour from the films explored in this chapter consist of mostly unpaid forms (e.g., pregnancy, childbirth, childcare, meal preparation, housecleaning, procreation, sex, and emotional support). These are also examples of invisible labour identified by socialist feminists involved in the global Wages for Housework movement of the 1970s (Dalla Costa [1972] 2016; Federici [1975] 2020b, [1975] 2020c, [1975] 2020a; James [1975] 2012).

Socialist feminists rejected capitalist imperatives and the exploitation of women's reproductive labour. According to their critiques, capitalism established an unequal "wage relation" between men and women and a hierarchy wherein invisible unpaid forms of labour (and those who performed them) were devalued, even though

"virtually all other activities are a preparation for work or a recuper-
ation from it" (James [1983] 2012, 149). As Selma James stated, "the
wage relation is not only a power relation between waged worker
and employer but between those workers who do and those workers who do not have wages. This is the material basis of the social
antagonism between the sexes" ([1983] 2012, 151). In other words,
capitalism and the commodified labour power upon which it rests is
underpinned by women's unrecognized labour. Moreover, these critiques contended that, even when women were employed in waged
labour, their work continued in a second shift at home.

Feminist themes related to reproductive labour run throughout
Rosemary's Baby and *The Stepford Wives*, and an analysis of these
texts can help us think critically about the ways in which they compared with the actual concerns articulated by feminist thinkers at
that time.

Setting the Scene

In the late 1960s and early 1970s, social roles and expectations for
women were shifting. Increasing numbers of women entered the
workforce, got divorced, or never got married, and many dealt
with husbands who were struggling with rapidly outmoded mas-
culinities (Gee and Jackson 2017). This was a time of change and
possibility, when new futures were imagined through civil rights
and global decolonization, anti-war, labour, counterculture, and
new left movements (Echols 2002).

The women's liberation movement, which also emerged during
this era, had gained salience by the late 1960s. Generally, the movement promoted consciousness raising about the objectification of
women and learned gender roles under patriarchy. More specifically, women's rights groups focused on reforming existing legal
and political systems; for example, in the United States, the National
Organization for Women (NOW) advocated for gender equality in
the workforce (Kretschmer 2019). Though not homogeneous, such
mainstream feminist groups often centred on white women's experiences and encouraged women to assume more economic agency

by pursuing equal rights in the workplace while unburdening themselves of oppressive domestic labour. This labour was often offloaded onto working-class women, immigrants, and women of colour, who did not see their experiences represented in mainstream feminist groups (Davis 1981; Taylor 2017; Combahee River Collective [1977] 2017; Third World Women's Alliance [1971] 2016).

While notable reformist figures such as Betty Friedan and Gloria Steinem are often widely associated with feminism of this era, socialist and radical feminists such as Mariarosa Dalla Costa, Selma James, Silvia Federici, and Beverly and Barbara Smith are less well remembered. Key works, such as Casey Hayden and Mary King's *Sex and Caste* ([1965] 2016), Shulamith Firestone and Anne Koedt's "The Red Stockings Manifesto" ([1968] 2016), Roxanne Dunbar's "Female Liberation as the Basis for Social Revolution" ([1969] 2016), and "The Combahee River Collective Statement" ([1977] 2017), critiqued the structural, inequitable relations between men and women under capitalism. They were influenced by the politics of leftist groups like Students for a Democratic Society and the Black Panthers and shared a capitalist critique with them. However, socialist and radical feminists recognized the gender inequality within these movements and more generally (Firestone 1970; Firestone and Koedt [1968] 2016; Echols 2002); therefore, they organized autonomously from such male-led groups (Taylor 2017).

The international Wages for Housework movement maintained that a public recognition of the invisible labour performed by women would enable them to opt out of it and would highlight the exploitative conditions of capitalism for waged and unwaged labourers (Federici [1975] 2020c; James [1972] 2012). Adapting approaches from Karl Marx ([1867] 1977) and Friedrich Engels ([1884] 2016) to focus on the unique exploitation of women under capitalism, Mariarosa Dalla Costa noted that "the oppression of women … did not begin with capitalism. What began with capitalism was more the intense exploitation of women as women" ([1972] 2016, 274). According to Dalla Costa, not only did the confinement of a woman to the home prevent her from organizing, it degraded her physical and intellectual integrity, turning her into a mere shadow of her husband, even when she worked outside the home for wages. As Dalla Costa explained, *"the capitalist function of the uterus ...* cuts off all her possibilities of creativity and of the development of her working activity, so it cuts off the expression of her sexual, psychological and emotional autonomy" (Dalla Costa [1972] 2016, 280, emphasis added).

Similarly, in grappling with the incongruencies between Marxist foundations and feminist critiques, Lise Vogel ([1983] 2013) argued that the dependency of capitalism (and not of the family unit) on the biological labour of women facilitates their exploitation. Critiques of women's exploitation because of their biological ability to reproduce capitalism as articulated by Vogel, Federici, and Dalla Costa echo throughout *Rosemary's Baby* and *The Stepford Wives* in horrific ways. Additionally, in the novels and filmic adaptations, both heroines eventually realize that, within their oppressive, patriarchal systems, meaningful relationships with their husbands are impossible, as they are based on gender and sex exploitation. Although they were perhaps not originally intended as capitalist critiques, we can extend Levin's texts in this way using the ideas of socialist feminist thinkers of their era.

Liberate Rosemary!

Rosemary's Baby (1968), based on Ira Levin's best-selling novel, published in 1967, is both widely revered as a ground-breaking film and infamous for the bizarre set of circumstances affiliated with it (Munn and Willoughby 2018). The urban legends that surround its production and much of the discussion of the film over the past fifty years are beyond the scope of this chapter. Yet, some important points of contextualization should be noted. First, while the story centres on evil dealings within the Bramford apartment building, feminist tensions at their height in the late 1960s are central themes throughout both the novel and film. Though gesturing towards a progressive feminist politics at the time, the film reflected the sexist and racist attitudes of both Levin and director Roman Polanski. For example, Levin sketched out Rosemary's character in a way that might encourage a victim-blame reading when she is raped and coerced by a satanic cult: "She likes sex, and would like a little more," and though she grew up Catholic, "she doesn't miss God at all" (Levin, as cited in Munn and Willoughby 2018, 21). The horrific rape scene in both the film and novel is also layered, as Polanski has become infamous for sexual assault across decades.[2] Yet these are not the only reasons these texts are problematic.

Though taking place in a racially diverse New York City, the book and film centre completely on white characters. There is only one Black character (played by D'Urville Martin) who makes a repeat appearance in the filmic version of *Rosemary's Baby* – as an elevator operator who also appears in a hallucination. In the book, the character is at first referred to as "a uniformed Negro boy," later identified as Diego, and he is mostly treated as a fixture of the elevator (Levin [1967] 2017, 6). The novel also refers to "Negro laundresses," whom Rosemary encounters in the basement of her building, but these characters are only briefly mentioned (28–9). The marginalization of Black characters engaged in reproductive labour in the book, and Rosemary's discomfort with them, illustrates the racist ubiquity of white identity of this era (Dyer 2005).[3] Moreover, the film indexes feminist themes only in relation to white women's experiences.

The film follows young married couple Rosemary and Guy Woodhouse (Mia Farrow and John Cassavetes), who are moving into their new apartment in the ominous Bramford building in New York City. Having children is referred to as Rosemary's "career" ambition, but Guy, an aspiring actor looking for acclaim and wealth, is much less enthusiastic about starting a family (Levin, as cited in Munn and Willoughby 2018, 21). While scholars and film critics have pointed out the increasing agency that Rosemary establishes as the story unfolds (Eyrenci 2013, 73) – for example, she cuts her hair into a short pixie-crop, to Guy's dismay – the power dynamic in the couple's relationship makes them an apt illustration of patriarchy. Guy's bravado and controlling nature is juxtaposed with Rosemary's submissiveness at the beginning of the film. Farrow's depiction of Rosemary is at first child-like and naive, and her petite frame, playfulness, and hyper-femininity reinforce this depiction. Guy earns and controls the couple's income and makes decisions about procreation, while Rosemary concerns herself with domestic labour and works tactically to have her needs and desires addressed. Their unequal power relation illustrates the problematic wage relations facilitated within capitalism (James [1983] 2012).

At the beginning of the film, Rosemary's primary function seems to be supporting her husband at home so that he may go to work: preparing his meals, providing emotional support, love making, and keeping and decorating their home. Seemingly "precapitalist" Rosemary acts as "only as a shadow behind the shoulders of the husband who goes out each day" (Dalla Costa [1972] 2016, 284), and, as Federici ([1975] 2020b) suggests, her "love" is a form of labour. Rosemary dotes on Guy and strokes his ego by proudly and repeatedly reciting his acting roles to anyone who will listen. In one scene, Guy returns home from work, and Rosemary rushes to greet him. She then promptly goes to the kitchen to fix him a sandwich and a beer. Along with these offerings, she comforts him with emotional labour and encouraging words when he tells her he did not get a coveted part in a production. As Federici notes, "hidden" affective labour such as emotional support can be counted among other forms of domestic work: "Housework is much more than house cleaning. It is servicing wage earners physically, emotionally, sexually, getting them ready for work day after day" ([1975] 2020a, 27). Guy's self-esteem is fragile, and he relies on Rosemary for support when he is particularly vulnerable. This relationship illustrates how, in the commodification of labour power, capitalists get two workers in the husband and wife, regardless of whether she also engages in wage labour. This wage relation is not merely a by-product, but underpins capitalism (James [1983] 2012, [1972] 2012).

Guy suddenly lands a starring role in a play after the lead actor mysteriously goes blind. Soon after, Rosemary is delighted when Guy, out of the blue, suggests they have a baby. He has even marked the calendar to note her most fertile days. Everything seems to be going well with the couple's plans for conception, but events take a sharp turn when Rosemary is drugged without her knowledge and has a series of bizarre hallucinations, which include visualizing a monstrous beast raping her. As the film goes on, it is clear that Guy has conspired with his neighbours to enrol Rosemary and their future family unit in a plot to advance his career. He agrees to exploit Rosemary's reproductive capacities quite literally by using her uterus as a way to achieve upward class mobility; he and his neighbours have orchestrated her rape by Satan and the birth of the devil incarnate through her. In the beginning of the book, Guy keeps track of Rosemary's menstrual cycle to avoid getting her pregnant, then later uses this same knowledge to facilitate her impregnation.

The violence experienced by Rosemary and lack of control over her own body and reproductive capacities, and therefore autonomy, reflected major points of concern for feminists. Many women sought economic stability and independence, which were enabled partly through oral contraception, which, in the United States, became legally available to married couples in 1965, and then to individuals regardless of marital status in 1973. At the same time, legal abortion became more readily available across the United States after the Supreme Court acknowledgment that abortion (like contraception) fell under the constitutional right to privacy (Reagan 1997).[4] However, struggles continue to try to protect and access these rights, as evidenced by the 2022 overturn of *Roe v. Wade* (Stollberg 2020; Totenberg and McCammon 2022).

Rosemary's rape and her response to it spoke to another key debate for feminists at that time. Without knowing the full scope of the horrific violence perpetrated against her – she believes it is Guy who has physically violated her – Rosemary is clearly disturbed: "Guy had taken her without her knowledge, had made love to her as a mindless body … rather than as the complete mind-and-body person she was" (Levin [1967] 2017, 104).[5] To add insult to injury, Guy wakes Rosemary the next morning to make him breakfast, slapping her on her buttock to get her out of bed. In the novel, even after the physical and psychic trauma of Rosemary's terrible violation, she gets out of bed, makes Guy breakfast, does the dishes, cleans the kitchen, makes the bed, and tidies the apartment. Guy's use of physical prodding is an indication that Rosemary, like other women performing housework, does not have control over her conditions of labour, hours, or the kind of work she must do (James [1952] 2012, 20); this forced labour and subordination is particularly insidious because it follows such shocking acts of violence and is couched in the expectation that, as a woman, Rosemary should feel obliged to perform it (Federici [1975] 2020b). Moreover, the simultaneous sexualization and infantilization accompanying the slap on the buttock illustrates Guy's treatment of Rosemary's body as his property – an idea that had legal support. While this might sound like a feminist nightmare, Rosemary's violent sexual exploitation and domestic labour were both part of a working understanding of marriage.

As Rebecca M. Ryan points out, the legal treatment of marriage as a "unity," which was rooted in eighteenth-century law, wherein a wife forfeited her legal existence to her husband, also guaranteed men "conjugal rights," "granting the husband authority over the wife's person economically and physically" (1995, 953). This treatment of women as subordinate in marriage manifested in the marital rape exemption, held up in most state laws until the late 1970s, when it was challenged by radical feminists (Brownmiller 1975) and eventually state courts.[6] As Federici asserts, state-condoned rape was not only used to control women, it also helped lay the foundations of capitalism, as it divided workers politically by pandering to men and prioritizing their individual rights (2014, 47). By the same token, women's coercion into reproducing labour power through literal reproduction and sexual labour also circumscribes their sexuality and encourages them to be content in their own exploitation by understanding it as love and wifely obligation (ibid.). Therefore, Rosemary's confusion over what happened to her could be partly explained by her desire to be a mother as well as by Guy's legal right to have sex with her whenever he chose, as her consent was implied under the law.

Rosemary's lack of control over her own body and reproduction, facilitating her dependence on Guy and the other Bramford residents, also makes it difficult for her to leave. As with the main protagonist in Levin's *Stepford Wives*, Rosemary's ability to organize against her oppressive circumstances is severely limited. She cannot move beyond the four walls of her home without close surveillance, and her pregnancy and lack of capital limit her mobility.

Figure 2.1. Rosemary tries to escape her oppressive conditions. Still from the film *Rosemary's Baby* (1968), directed by Roman Polanski and released by Paramount Pictures. Photo by SydBarrettDragon via Flickr. CC BY 2.0: https://creativecommons.org/licenses/by/2.0/

Rosemary is presented with a choice at the end, once the baby is born, albeit a Hobson's choice with a high degree of coercion. The Bramford residents implore Rosemary to be a mother to the baby. While at first she is repulsed, Rosemary reluctantly approaches the cradle, and the final shot shows her smiling and looking down tenderly. Though the ending is ambiguous in the film, one could easily infer that Rosemary has decided to raise the child (Levin [1967] 2017, 267). As with Levin's later novel, Rosemary's fate has in part been decided by her choice to enter into a coercive set of social relations or a "sexual contract" (R. Ryan 1995) – that of wife/mother – in which she is now trapped. Yet socialist feminists would have argued that it was not merely patriarchy, but capitalism that shaped social relations. Therefore, the idea that one could opt out of such relations by avoiding marriage and motherhood was misguided.

"Holy Cow!": Consciousness Raising with the Stepford Wives

Like *Rosemary's Baby*, *The Stepford Wives* is filled with timely references to the opportunities, tensions, and contradictions of feminist currents. The 1972 novel by Ira Levin and the 1975 film directed by Bryan Forbes take place in a Connecticut suburb called Stepford, an enclave of mostly white professional men and their families. Heroine Joanna Eberhart has moved there with her two young children at the behest of her husband, Walter, who is a lawyer. She is ambivalent about the move and the side-lining of her burgeoning career as a photographer. Unlike Rosemary, Joanna is more legible as a mainstream feminist vis-à-vis the popular tropes she exhibits. She repeatedly dismisses women overburdened with domestic labour as "hausfraus," despite the fact that she does most of the domestic work in her own home, from childcare to entertaining her husband's friends as they ogle her. In the book, there are several references to Betty Friedan, NOW, and women's liberation, with which Joanna notes being involved.

The identification of Joanna and her best friend, Bobbie, as feminists, referencing their connection with popular movements of that era (and also through aesthetic markers like bralessness),[7] establishes a context for the stark binary with Stepford women, who wholeheartedly embrace their submissive role and whose husbands reign supreme. Both kinds of characters seem to be stock depictions of largely white and heteronormative mainstream second wave feminists and their counterparts in conservative circles who embraced and lobbied for conventional gender roles. To Joanna's surprise, most of the women she meets in Stepford seem solely interested in domestic chores and pleasing their husbands, never even pausing to socialize. This is expressed in a comment by the character Carole Van Sant (Nanette Newman), who "cooks as good as she looks."[8] When asked if she is happy in her limited role as a housewife, Carole states, "Ted is doing really well in his scientific research now, and I give him a good home. I really think that helps."

While the Stepford women labour at home, waxing their floors until they shine, baking, and watching the children, their husbands spend their leisure hours at the Men's Association, the men-only club where they network with neighbours and other professionals. Over the course of the novel, Joanna discovers that the Men's Association had been formed shortly after a well-attended talk by Betty Friedan for the Stepford Women's Association. Both the Women's Association and the League of Women Voters have since been inactive, with their leaders abandoning all forms of women's organizing, aside from the garden club.

Joanna notices her friends, one by one, become like the other women of Stepford, even changing in appearance – they look much the same, but with enhanced feminine features (e.g., larger breasts), undergarments, and makeup – and their conversations sound like actresses in commercials praising the quality of their cleaning products. One humorous gesture towards women's liberation depicted in the film is an attempt by Joanna and Bobbie to organize the women of Stepford to attend a consciousness-raising session about their exploitation and to help unlearn gender. Women's liberation feminists saw sexism as a pervasive part of everyday culture, where "centuries of a male-dominated gender system had been more internalized, imbedding in many women (and men) the assumption that women's subordination was natural" (L. Gordon 2013, 23). However, Joanna and Bobbie fail in their efforts. "Holy Cow!" remarks Bobbie in disbelief, as a serious conversation about whether the women are fulfilled is met with emphatic endorsements of Easy On Spray Starch.

It is eventually revealed that the Stepford men have conspired to replace their wives with domestic androids who provide for their every need. Noted throughout the film are the now enhanced sex lives of the association men, which ostensibly makes them into more confident professionals by boosting their self-esteem. After-all, their wives, who worship them, have few needs to which they must attend, save an occasional tune-up, and they will not complain about their exploitative working conditions. The children of Stepford also do not seem to mind their mothers' newly pleasant dispositions. Their remade mothers seem to embody the one-sided relationality that Virginia Woolf (1937) described as "the angel in the house."

Figure 2.2. "Not only would I do it, I'd do it for free." The Stepford wives embrace their gendered and sexual exploitation. Carole Mallory and Toni Reid in *The Stepford Wives*, 1975. Everett Collection/Alamy Stock Photo.

At the end of *The Stepford Wives* filmic version, a young Black couple moves into the mostly white neighbourhood, likely a reference to a slightly more prominent character in the book, Ruthanne Hendry, though the film spends no time developing these characters. In the book, Ruthanne's husband, Royal, has joined the Men's Association. Perhaps the lesson learned with *The Stepford Wives* is that the lure of the American dream, and upward class mobility, will absorb and assimilate difference, reproducing a family unit dependent on gender and sex exploitation regardless of race. But, while making nods to people of colour, white women's experiences are treated as ubiquitous in *The Stepford Wives*, as they were within second wave feminism itself.

Some scholars have celebrated *The Stepford Wives* as "feminist" (Foertsch 2019, 102), and Levin alludes to feminist currents throughout the book and quotes Simone de Beauvoir on its cover. However, it is unclear where the novel leaves the reader vis-à-vis a feminist orientation. In commenting on the book, horror novelist Peter Straub noted that he was uncertain whether it "can properly be called a feminist satire" (2002, xiii). Betty Friedan, who is referenced several times throughout the novel as the catalyst for the formation of the Men's Association, described *The Stepford Wives* as a "rip-off" of the women's movement (Foertsch 2019, 112).

It is also unclear whether Levin has concluded that women's liberation is of no use in the face of patriarchy. The book points out that Joanna's friends have set aside their own interests in favour of being wives and mothers, and even her friend who opted to have a career "had been passed up for a promotion she damn well knew she deserved" ([1972] 1998, 51). While Joanna insists she will never become an "asking-to-be exploited patsy" like the "hausfrau" who lives next door, she, like all the women around her in the suburbs, will become a Stepford wife (9). This seems to be a condemnation of marriage and the suburbs, which Friedan referred to as "the comfortable concentration camp" (Echols 2002, 106). It has been noted that Levin was himself living in a suburb and going through a divorce while writing the book (Foertsch 2019; Kampel, 2007).

Whether Levin is critiquing patriarchy is also uncertain. Is he suggesting that it is just men's nature to be sexist, and is he ultimately an apologist for it? Though Joanna states in the first pages of the book that her husband is interested in women's issues and that "lots of men are," she is clearly mistaken (3). Perhaps Levin implies that no men are actually feminists and that they will trade in their wives for a robot wearing their mother's perfume any day.[9] Perhaps both the novel and filmic adaptations indicate that reform within the family unit is impossible, as husbands – even those who, according to their wives, are feminists – cannot be trusted to act in good faith. However, while Levin reduces feminism to consciousness raising about gender roles and a rejection of domestic work, and attributes men's bad behaviour to sexism, *The Stepford Wives* misses concerns over the wage relations that make antagonism between Joanna and her husband inevitable.

Patriarchy and More

To return to the quotation in the title of this chapter: Joanna was correct that the Stepford men were behind the conspiracy against their wives, just as Guy was behind the plot to entrap Rosemary. However, by framing patriarchy as a conscious plot by men, we miss another important critique: that all of our relationships and social institutions are shaped at least in part by our conditions of production and reproduction. The main protagonists of *Rosemary's Baby* and *The Stepford Wives* exist within a social relation wherein their own labour will always be devalued in the hierarchy of wage earners (their husbands). Even if they did earn a wage, these women would still be exploited because of their capacity to reproduce labour power (whether that reproduction is biological or not), producing and caring for the next generation of workers through emotional, sexual, and physical labour. In Rosemary's case, she may encounter a change in relative social status in relation to the other building residents if she acquiesces to motherhood, but can never fully escape her conditions. In contrast, Joanna is replaced by a worker who will not protest or organize against her oppressive working conditions. Knowledge of their exploitation and nods to women's liberation does little to help either woman.

Perhaps these dystopic tales marked a growing disenchantment with second wave feminism and Levin's articulation of its impossibility. As the character Carole Van Sant remarks in *The Stepford Wives* following her transformation from feminist to content homemaker, "We weren't accomplishing anything useful." This disavowal undermines the revolutionary potential of feminism; moreover, depictions of feminism as centred on consciousness raising, even if satire, painted feminist movements in a reductive way, missing their more substantive critiques.

However, despite the fact that Levin's novels and their film adaptations missed these larger points of feminist thinkers and centred largely on white women, they were effective in illustrating the deeply entrenched manipulation in expecting reproductive labour be done out of "love" and pointed to the coercive nature of this sentiment. As Federici notes, this "love" is one-sided "unwaged work" ([1975] 2020b, 11). But, just recognizing such labour, and perhaps even compensating it, is not enough to challenge the coercive system of oppression that it enables. James, Federici, and other socialist feminists of the Wages for Housework movement hoped this recognition would spark a deeper economic and social revolution. Instead, as discussed in the next chapter, mediated mothers after the second wave shifted their wage relations by entering the workforce, but they were expected to do so without structural supports in a "post-feminist" context.

chapter three

Mother Hustle: Entrepreneurial Motherhood in Home Renovation and Design Television

"An independent woman who makes her own money and feeds her self [sic] and family ... basically a female baller."

("Hustler girl," urbandictionary.com)

The entrepreneurial mother of the home design reality television show has come to be a widely recognized convention. She and her husband often have a rags-to-riches story in which they were "ordinary people" who got their start in house flipping or home renovation when they were discovered by reality television producers (Dekel 2015), sometimes with the help of a large social media following (Schmidt 2021). While the home makeover mom is in charge of aesthetics and design, her husband is generally handy, and sometimes a contractor who does the heavy lifting, or he attends to the business side of things (e.g., on *Masters of Flip*, *Island of Bryan*, and *Dream Home Makeover*). Every now and then, their children enter the picture in carefully edited and orchestrated scenes to remind viewers that the star of the show is a mom (who works). During their appearances, the family pretends they are engaged in quality time rather than the immaterial labour of reality television (Andrejevic 2004).

Within these shows, performances of motherhood are synergized and integrated across different product lines, businesses, reality television spin-offs, and media platforms.[1] For example, reality television stars Chip and Joanna Gaines used their success starring with their children on the HGTV show *Fixer Upper* to start their own local businesses in Waco, Texas; to grow a national construction and design company, a home decor line, and a magazine; and to launch their own home and garden network. Perhaps the pinnacle of their branding success, Magnolia Network distributes content internationally and is co-owned by the Gaineses with Warner Brothers Discovery and overseen by HBO (Zhan 2022). In short, entrepreneurial motherhood in home design reality TV is big business.

Within brands such as that built by Joanna Gaines, spouses and children play a central role. The appearance of children not only signifies a heteronormative, atomized family unit, it also reminds viewers that the star can "do it all" if she just invests enough labour in her personal brand. Children are enrolled in their mothers' brands where both unpaid reproductive labour and paid labour meld together, and the actual *labour* of reproductive labour is largely concealed but gestured toward. Also concealed is the broader lack of access to structural supports like affordable childcare and parental leave, while the disproportionate total work burden performed by mothers is naturalized.

Such reality television shows are distributed in Canada through international networks, and many were produced in Canada with the support of private and public funding (e.g., *Masters of Flip, Making It Home with Kortney and Dave*, and *Island of Bryan*). Although the focus of this chapter is on motherhood in home design and makeover reality television shows appearing in Canada on HGTV Canada and Discovery+, the shows and brands discussed are designed to be exported widely to maximize profit. Such distribution leads to the proliferation of a post-feminist (Gill 2007) brand of neoliberal motherhood marked by precarious and "flexible" labour (Hearn 2009; Wilson and Chivers Yochim 2017; Watson 2020) and illustrates the ways in which national cultural policy is invested in international flows of capital in promoting Canadian cultural products. The resulting performance of motherhood, wherein mothers are responsible for seamlessly traversing both domains of paid and unpaid labour while constantly hustling, imposes impossible expectations for those engaged in motherwork with few or no structural supports. In home renovation shows, this inequity is reinforced by a system that also disadvantages minorities and those of a lower socio-economic status (Bjornholt 2020; Cobble 2004), while privileging white homeownership and wealth accumulation and responsibilizing mothers with their maintenance.

The Promotional and Flexible Self and Home

The trajectory of the enterprising home and garden reality television star working hard to build a personal brand for upward social mobility is not unique. As Ouellette and Hay (2008) point out, it follows a longer, individualistic Western ethos centred on personal improvement, and is reflected in other reality television shows (see also T. Lewis, 2009). However, the intensification and ubiquity of the personal brand is unique in late modern capitalism, in which "the worker puts his or her own life experience, communicative competency, and self into the job" to create a promotional self-brand in the face of precarious working conditions where they are required to be "flexible" with the market (Hearn 2009, 56). Accompanied by a lack of permanence and paid work security, these conditions fluctuate with the fickleness of market demand, where every aspect of a worker's life is potentially commodified. While the invisible and highly manicured around-the-clock maintenance of the personal brand is obscured, this "flexible" labour is celebrated as a form of choice. As Hearn argues with respect to makeover reality television shows, where one's personal brand is often seen as a means to employment, "the message of self-branding narrated and produced on transformation television ultimately exacerbates the very conditions of personal and material insecurity it claims to address" (2009, 55). If an individual cannot make it within this entrepreneurial hustle because their self-brand is not strong enough, then, by extension of this logic, they simply are not hustling hard enough.

The home and garden lifestyle genre tends to valorize a middleclass sensibility that emphasizes wealth accumulation through real estate while omitting the dire economic conditions many people face. According to the Canada Mortgage and Housing Corporation (CMHC), "for many Canadians, homeownership represents a key tool for wealth accumulation. An increasing body of literature finds that generational wealth, mainly accumulated through housing, explains differences in current inequality rates" (CMHC 2021a). A 2021 report by the CMHC using national census and survey data revealed major discrepancies between white homeownership and that of racial minorities, with Black, Arab, Indigenous, and Latinx people experiencing the lowest rates of homeownership, and with the gap widening between 2006 and 2016. At 44.5 per cent, the rate of homeownership among Black Canadians in 2016 was well below the national average of 72.6 per cent (CMHC 2021b).

While homeownership is beyond the realm of possibility for many people, the hyper-focus on it as an investment reproduces an anxiety over market value for those who can own homes. As Rosenberg (2011) argues, the broad aesthetic concerns of home makeover reality television are based on ideas of resale value and increasing profit rather than personalization. For example, drawing on the aesthetic of "soft modernism," colour palates in such shows are generally very neutral and soothing, and furniture and artwork rather unobjectionable and never too "ethnic." Furniture, fixtures, textiles, and knick-knacks are designed to appeal widely and thus to help increase the value of the home for an imagined universal buyer. Gender roles help in the maintenance and prescription of these rather white aesthetics in several ways.

Women have long turned to television shows for instruction and expertise within the domestic domain, with the aim of self-improvement and building cultural capital (Spigel 2009). As Lunt states, "such programs provide an important site for the expression of taste and expertise that responds to the emerging needs of lifestyle consumption" (2008, 98). In the Canadian context, the notion that home improvement shows fit into the educational/self-improvement realm is reflected in the broadcast licence for HGTV Canada, which promised "programming that presents practical, hands-on advice and instruction about homes and gardens" (as cited in Bruce 2009, 79). Behaviour is modelled on such shows by experts who demonstrate how viewers can engage in perpetual self-improvement. An important aspect of this modelled behaviour is to know the proper aesthetic cues (Bourdieu 1987) as well as what Skeggs (2009) describes as a moral economy. This moral economy is rooted in a middle-class (white) aesthetic, and individuals of a lower socio-economic status are shamed for not reflecting this norm and are expected to internalize the discourse of self-improvement through the makeover (Sender 2006).

The moral economy of home improvement has particular implications for mothers balancing various forms of labour. Because home renovation and improvement shows fit within the parameters of a profit-driven framework of international media conglomerates, motherhood is constructed within very narrow parameters and commodified so that it will appeal across markets, from the most conservative to the more moderate. This produces a performance of motherhood in which mothers are always working, and every aspect of their lives is fair game for commodification, from their families to their bathrooms. Everything must be clean, look sleek and modern, or intentionally distressed or dishevelled: audiences cannot see the children messing things up, and the actual process and duration of childrearing cannot be visible, though children must occasionally make an appearance or be mentioned. Mothers must also look very "put together" and heteronormatively attractive to match their tasteful design aesthetic, a point reinforced by filtered and well-lit shots as well as perfect hair and makeup. Their spouses are also ever-present, and successes are generally in relation to that of husbands in some way, as evidenced by their duo partnership – he's often sitting next to, and interviewed side-by-side with, her (as on *Fixer Upper*, *Dream Home Makeover*, and *Masters of Flip*). More importantly, motherhood in these shows includes heavy lifting in brand building. Not only must mothers increase the value of their homes and those of others, they must learn to synergize their various endeavours and stretch their brands across multiple goods and services, from home renovation firms to self-help books, home decor lines, and product placements where their role as mother becomes an integral part of their brand.

Motherhood and the Reality of Reproductive Labour

Motherhood has seen a great deal of theorization since second wave feminism and since Adrienne Rich (1976) famously drew a distinction between practices and experiences of mothering and the institution of patriarchal motherhood in *Of Women Born*. Following theorists of maternal practice (O'Reilly 2020; Collins 1994), this chapter assumes that motherwork extends beyond essentialized roles, "to anyone who does the work of mothering as a central part of her or his life" (O'Reilly 2020, 51). However, it is important to note that in most countries, including Canada and the United States, reproductive labour is largely gendered and disproportionately shouldered by women (Waring 1988).

Women's expansion into waged labour since the Second World War has not meant a reduction in reproductive labour, but has compounded it (Richardson 2020). Over the past several decades, data on total work burden and time use related to gender in Canada has revealed additional pressures placed on women. As Moyser and Burlock (2018) note in their analysis of data collected through the General Social Survey on Time Use (1986, 2010, 2015) as well as the General Social Survey on Caregiving and Care Receiving (2012), while both men and women now spend more time with their children compared with thirty years ago, women have increased their time more than men; compared to men, women in Canada perform more childcare, are more likely to do unpaid work, and are more likely to do housework as both a primary task and as an activity undertaken while multitasking.[2]

Women spent 6.3 more hours than men doing housework each week; even when working in paid labour, women continue to do a disproportionate amount of housework. As Mosyer and Burlock (2018) found, women tend to do more labour at home when not engaged in paid labour, whereas men, on average, tend to do the same amount of labour at home regardless of the number of hours they spend in paid work. Women in Canada spent an average of 1.5 hours more than men per day on unpaid work as a primary activity. This disproportionate labour has an impact on women's "heightened perceptions of time pressure" (Mosyer and Burlock 2018, 5; Watson 2020).

As these statistics indicate, the right to paid work outside the home, which was a major concern of second wave feminism, has not, in and of itself, been the answer to maternal empowerment (Buzzanell et al. 2019; Briggs 2018). This is especially the case when paid work is precarious and comes with little flexibility or control over hours and working conditions; no benefits, security, paid, or parental leave; low pay; little respect; and unaffordable childcare (Davis 1981; Buzzanell et al. 2019). This inequity extends to pink-collar workers who provide childcare for middle- and upper-class parents, and who largely experience precarious working conditions and difficulty accessing affordable childcare themselves (Buzzanell et al. 2019). Those who perform domestic labour and childcare are disproportionately women, people of colour, those of lower socio-economic status, and newcomers (Anderson and Moore 2014; Duffy 2007).

These barriers to paid work are paired with the direct competition mothers are placed in with other labourers to be productive under neoliberal conditions that assume a generic worker who has no caregiving responsibilities and who can work an eight-hour shift or more (Lewis 2006). In this system, mothers are more likely to face impoverishment, and a societal refusal to acknowledge their uneven conditions places them in an unreasonable double-bind that expects them to be adaptable and find workarounds (Richardson 2020). As Vandenbeld Giles notes, "mothers are encouraged to financialize the domestic space through 'work-from-home' ideals despite precariousness and often poor remuneration. Yet within the neoliberal framework, this creative 'freedom' only applies to a privileged sector of the population" (2020, 272). Given discourses around free choice and the conditions of neoliberal policies, which have "offloaded the costs and responsibilities of social reproduction onto families, women, and especially mothers," "mompreneurs" do not see a reduction in the number of hours they work but find ways to reconfigure their total work burden (Anderson and Moore 2014, 95, 96). Through the extension of the logics of "flexible labour," mothers who have the privilege to do so not only work from home, but also bring their home to work, folding their children into their paid labour, a practice that is naturalized through reality television.

Flipping as a Family Business: From Ontario to Nashville and Back Again

Kortney and Dave Wilson in many ways helped establish the groundwork for the reality television sub-genre featuring families enmeshed in home design and renovation. Prior to the success of *Masters of Flip* (2015–19), a four season show starring the married couple, which first appeared on W Network and HGTV Canada, the Wilsons starred in other shorter-lived reality television shows distributed in Canada and the United States. *Meet the Wilsons*, a 2009 CMT Canada show, focused on the couple's struggles raising their young children, pursuing careers in Nashville as country music performers, and making ends meet early in their home renovation careers. A 2009 *CanWestNews* article described *Meet the Wilsons* in the following way: "Imagine a full crew behind you when you're filming the kids' birthdays, family vacations, even changing the diapers. *Meet The Wilsons* is a kind of Truman Show about workaday Nashville folk trying to juggle music careers with the demands of raising a family" (Shaw 2009).

The Wilsons Flip Out (2011) continued to follow the family as Kortney and Dave further developed their skills in house flipping as their music careers faltered. A promotional photo for the show pictures the family in matching coveralls and intentionally dishevelled hair, with Kortney holding their youngest child, just a toddler at the time. The children were absent from the later, better-known, *Masters of Flip*, although they were referenced periodically, and the Wilsons' dynamic as a married couple was a key feature of that show. The children reappeared in *Making It Home with Kortney and Dave* (2020), in which the couple worked with clients to renovate their homes. It marked their last collaboration, as the Wilsons had announced their separation in 2019 (Samhan 2019). In 2021, the show was renamed *Making It Home with Kortney and Kenny*. In it, Kortney appeared without Dave but alongside co-host and contractor Kenny Brain, a former contestant on Global Television's reality TV show *Big Brother Canada*, also owned by parent company Corus Entertainment.

In addition to commodifying their family experiences onscreen, the Wilsons found a way to marry private and public financial support by tapping into Canadian cultural policy and financing. While *Masters of Flip* was set primarily in Nashville, Tennessee, and distributed internationally, the Wilsons were born in Ontario, and their shows were produced by Canadian production companies, Rhino Productions/Corus Studios, and Scott Brothers Entertainment, founded by *Property Brothers* celebrities Drew and Jonathan Scott (also Canadians). Canadian regulations, including those of the Canadian Radio-television and Telecommunications Commission (CRTC), benefited the Wilsons' shows. The aim of the CRTC, to ensure that Canadian broadcasters have the responsibility to "promote Canadian talent and successes here and abroad" (Bruce 2009, 80), helped ensure that, however loosely defined, a certain percentage of Canadian home improvement and renovation "talent" would make it onto Canadian screens. *Masters of Flip* was supported by financing from the Canadian government as well as provincial and private funding, including from the Ontario Media Development Corporation, otherwise known as Ontario Creates, which operates under the provincial Ministry of Tourism, Culture and Sport.[3]

In addition, the show was supported by the National Bank of Canada TV and Motion Picture Finance Group and the Bell Fund. *Masters of Flip* and the later show starring the Wilsons also included sponsorships from private corporations such as Vista-Print, Behr Paints, Home Depot, Telus, and The Brick.[4] These private/public initiatives helped push Canadian cultural products in a competitive national and international market. As Wagman (2002) discusses, such enterprises underpin aspects of Canadian nation-building, with special privileges and nationalist affinities for private enterprises that support these efforts.

This early production support in Canada helped *Masters of Flip* cross over into international circulation: it was available in 90 territories by 2016 and 148 territories by 2017, through sales negotiated by Corus Entertainment, owners of W Network and HGTV Canada (PR Newswire, 2016, 2017). Despite the subtle Canadian undertones of the show, which are most likely discerned by fellow Canadians, a major contribution to the international success of *Masters of Flip* was its ability to reproduce a conventional family dynamic. This helped to ensure that the show was accepted not only in Canada (Canadians love their celebrities who have achieved international success)[5] but also in the United States, aided by the show's setting in the southern states. The Wilsons' background as country music performers in a fairly conventional, heteronormative family helped ensure that it would appeal in more conservative quarters. As if addressing such conservatism head on, Kortney Wilson states during the opening sequence of *Masters of Flip*, "he's my husband first, and he's my business partner second" (season 1, episode 1 A [Wilkes 2015a]).

Not only does the show centre on a married couple, it reflects conventional gender roles, as Kortney deals with design and aesthetics and Dave addresses budgeting and coordinates construction. This formula is repeated in many similar shows, like *Fixer Upper*, *Island of Bryan*, and *Home Town*. However, there is some nuance in *Masters of Flip*. In keeping with the discourse of postfeminism, Kortney Wilson defies traditional gender roles in several ways. First, Kortney, not Dave, is decidedly the star of the show, and she frequently provides direction to Dave and the mostly cisgender male–presenting construction crew. She also helps in some aspects of the "heavy lifting," most notably during demolition. Moreover, as she notes in the opening sequence, she is a "licensed real estate professional," who negotiates the acquisition, marketing, and sales of properties. As with many post-feminist texts, throughout each episode, investment and profit are major themes. Each episode begins and concludes with the couple running the numbers to see how much potential profit they might gain by renovating and selling a particular house, and Kortney's designs play a key role in this process.

While *Masters of Flip* clearly demarcates Kortney Wilson's professional role, and the children do not appear in this show, HGTV's promotional materials centre on the couple's relationship and children (Grande 2019). The Wilson children are also referenced periodically in the show. For example, in an episode from season 1, after picking out the granite for a countertop, Kortney mentions she needs to leave, stating, "I have to go pick up the kids from gymnastics" (season 1, episode 9 [Wilkes 2015b]). Dave mentions the kids in the same episode, joking that they could save money by having them paint one of the rooms. At the end of the same season, the couple races to flip a house in time for their family vacation. At the end of the episode, which wraps up season 1, the Wilsons and their children, presumably on vacation, are pictured in a still shot (season 1, episode 12 [Wilkes 2015c]).

Season 1 of the subsequent show, *Making It Home with Kortney and Dave* (2020), features their children more prominently. At the beginning of each episode, the couple spend time with their children while they discuss clients they will introduce later in the episode. For example, the family is pictured eating breakfast, together at the beach, and crafting on the porch. It is important to situate this show in the context of *Fixer Upper* (2013–18), discussed further in the next section, which had seen major success prior to the start of *Making It Home with Kortney and Dave*. Perhaps taking its cue from this success, the latter assumes a strikingly similar format, starting each episode with their children and centring much more on families generally, as the couple mostly works with homeowners who have children or plan to grow their families. This family theme is a departure from the more profit-driven emphasis in *Masters of Flip*; as Kortney states in the *Making It Home* season 1 introduction, they are "helping other families figure out how to reno, where to save, and where to splurge" (season 1, episode 1 [Simard 2020]). In this season, Kortney frequently emotes with her clients and creates surprises for their children, and she is seen holding the children and babies of her clients.

Even after Kortney announced her separation from Dave on Instagram (Samhan 2019) and appeared in the revamped *Making It Home with Kortney and Kenny*, the families of clients continued to be a major focus of the show, and Kortney continued to emote heavily with them, tearing up when they cry and continuing to hold other people's babies and share photos of them. But the Wilson children no longer appeared, and Kortney infrequently referenced them or her role as a mother. Therefore, in *Making It Home With Kortney and Kenny*, Kortney performs motherwork through her maternal performance with other families.

The appearance and disappearance of the Wilson children evokes reproductive labour but also hides and commodifies it, employing family as part of a marketing strategy when it seems advantageous to do so. This model of the commodification of family life, which the Wilsons developed in their early reality television successes like *The Wilsons Flip Out*, has stretched even further through the mega brand built by Chip and Joanna Gaines.[6]

Bringing Baby to the Worksite

"I do one of those wraps – he's just with me in meetings. Yesterday we were in a meeting and he had a blowout. There were like 10 people sitting in the room, and he had a blowout, and I was like 'I gotta go. I'll be right back.' But I love it."
(Joanna Gaines on bringing her newborn to work, *Today*, 2018)

Joanna Gaines is being interviewed by Jenna Bush Hager, *Today Show* correspondent and daughter of former Republican president George W. Bush. The two sit on the porch of Gaines's family farmhouse in Waco, Texas. Gaines has given birth to her fifth child, now four months old, and is promoting her new home decor self-help book, *Homebody*. Hager and the other *Today Show* commentators back in the studio are effusive in their admiration for the reality television star who got her start on HGTV's *Fixer Upper* with her husband, Chip. Interspersed are images of Gaines holding her newborn and pictures of her other children frolicking in the agrarian setting of Waco. As Hager and Gaines tour the home, they reach the laundry room, and the latter comments that this is her favourite room in the house. It is *her* space, where she gets a lot of her writing and thinking done. She comments, "If you have to do a chore anyway," indicating that the actual work of writing (including her book, it is implied) happens simultaneously with her doing the family's laundry. Gaines continues, "It's so important that we create a space that's ours." Hager comments, "It's kind of like your woman cave" (*Today* 2018). Neither seem to register the irony that a "man cave" is usually a space for leisure and relaxation, and that this space where Joanna does the intellectual work of paid labour is entrenched in domestic labour, despite the fact that she is the centre of a very profitable transnational brand and media franchise.

The blurring of Joanna Gaines's domestic labour with paid labour in this segment is in keeping with the Gaines's family-friendly, Christian "powerhouse brand" (Meredith Corporation 2022, 2). It is also consistent with the particularly conservative region of the United States where they live and the show *Fixer Upper* was based. On the show, Joanna frequently wore T-shirts adorned with city or state logos, aligning her own identity with that of the region. The couple also signifies their membership within the community by referencing other business owners and members of their church (e.g., season 1, episode 9 [Matsumoto 2014d]). In addition to their growing real estate business and work renovating run-down properties into middle- and upper-class homes, the Gaines own businesses in Waco and have converted industrial farmland into a trendy shopping district. They have transformed "the Silos" into a focal point and "tourist Mecca," which 50,000 tourists visited each week in 2019 following the success of *Fixer Upper* (Petersen 2019). This transformation has not been good news for all existing residents, some of whom now struggle to meet the rising prices that come with gentrification (Petersen 2019). The rebranding of the town and the merchandise sold in and around the Silos are all on brand with Gaines's country chic aesthetic, from "boutiques with cute linen rompers" to towels inscribed "Alexa, please feed the kids," and pennants with the motto "Let go and Let God" (Petersen 2019, para. 1). The Magnolia brand, largely centred on Joanna Gaines, has proven successful nationally and internationally. In addition to the couple's home design and renovation firm, they have collectively created a home decor line sold through Target, among other retailers; starred in multiple reality television spinoff shows; written several books; and publish *Magnolia Journal* magazine, which boasts a readership of 5.4 million, 80 per cent of whom own their own homes (Meredith Corporation 2022).

Perhaps the pinnacle of the Gaines's brand, one in keeping with Oprah Winfrey's OWN model, is Magnolia Network, a cable network that is a joint venture between the Gaines and Discovery, Inc.

and overseen by HBO. While the show *Fixer Upper* reached sixteen million Canadian viewers alone, Magnolia Network and its business partners will potentially allow the Gaines's brand to stretch even further to new Canadian audiences (Corus 2022). Launched in Canada in March 2022 through Discovery+, the network bills itself as "TV that feels like home," with "family-friendly and unscripted" lifestyle programming related to home design and food (Corus 2022). In addition to streaming existing episodes of *Fixer Upper*, the network will feature the couple in a new, rebooted version, *Fixer Upper: Welcome Home*, and Joanna Gaines will appear in other programming, like *The Retro Plant Shop with Mikey and Jo*.

In all of these endeavors, family is central to making Joanna Gaines relatable to her fans. In HGTV's *Fixer Upper*, references to the Gaines's children and Joanna's role as a mother and wife feature prominently in the show. In the opening scenes of each episode, Chip and Joanna are pictured with their children, usually on the family farm. The family-centric branding starts from the very beginning of season 1: in the opening sequence, Joanna and Chip introduce themselves and the premise of the show as helping people get into *that* neighbourhood (the one with the good commutes and schools and expensive houses). Chip states that, over the past eight years, they've had four children and renovated over a hundred homes. In another sequence, the children accompany Chip and Joanna during a renovation; Joanna pulls one of her small children out of the way as Chip pries a fireplace mantle off the wall, with Joanna remarking, "Look at how strong he is" (season 1, episode 1 [Matsumoto 2013]. In this, and almost all aspects of the show, the couple assume very conventional gender roles, with Chip doing the heavy lifting, and Joanna making the design choices.

In the first episode of *Fixer Upper*, they help young, white-coded, heteronormative couple Doug and Lacey purchase a "fixer-upper" home so that they can move into an upper-middle-class neighbourhood (Castle Heights) that they could not otherwise afford. Both work at Baylor University, and, while they do not yet have children, Lacey comments that they plan to in the future. At the end of the episode, after Chip and Joanna have transformed their home, Doug and Lacey are pictured toasting with another white-coded couple, one of whom says, "Welcome to the neighbourhood." Doug and Lacey have realized their upward mobility through this middle-class dream: improve the value of your home and get ahead. Several times throughout the episode, Chip, Joanna, and Doug mention resale value, and they make decisions based on envisioning what buyers might expect in the future, should the couple sell the home. For example, when Chip and Joanna encourage the couple to upgrade their wiring, she comments, "When updating the electrical and the fixtures, this helps the resale value of the house" (season 1, episode 1 [Matsumoto 2013]). Though mention of profit is not as overt or as crass as in *Masters of Flip*, the idea of increasing the market value of homes is an underlying theme throughout *Fixer Upper*.

The appearance of their children, while not seamless, certainly seems manageable and fun. In this first episode and others, as they toggle childcare during renovations, Joanna informs Chip that the babysitter needs to leave. Later, as she's getting ready to style the home, Joanna again negotiates childcare with her husband: "If I could just get a couple hours alone to do this, that would be great." As is common throughout the series, Joanna fits her paid labour into her regular schedule of reproductive labour, while, presumably, Chip and others watch the children. Joanna is then seen alone in the house, adding the final, decorative touches before it is revealed to the clients. Joanna comments on the stress that she experiences from the pressures of her various roles in the same episode: "I'm stressed. I have ulcers in my mouth all the time. But I love my life." She makes the same kind of statement later in the season, in the context of all the different "hats" she needs to wear, "as the employer, as designer, as a mom, as the wife" (season 1, episode 2 [Matsumoto 2014a]). As with the opening quotation in this section, this refrain – that she feels the weight of her total work burden, but she loves it – is consistently made by Joanna Gaines. In other words, this is characterized as personal choice rather than as reflecting a lack of systemic support.

In other episodes, when Joanna is relieved of her childcare duties so that she can do the work of staging homes, she requests that Chip bring their children back to visit: "Can you bring me dinner and bring those kiddos by?" (season 1, episode 5 [Matsumoto 2014b]).

Of this choice, she states, "the second they walk in the door everything just shuts off for me creatively and I'm a mom." The Gaines children frequently visit client homes, even when they are staging, with Joanna telling them not to mess anything up (season 1, episode 6 [Matsumoto 2014c]). In such instances, Joanna has access to childcare but opts not to use it. In the last season of the show, the audience gets to view a rare, candid comment from the youngest daughter, Ella, expressing her feelings about being onscreen. Earlier footage shows that even when Chip and Joanna were onscreen being interviewed, they sometimes had their youngest daughter standing between them, clinging to their legs, just below and off camera. Joanna asks her daughter whether she wants to be on camera, to which Ella replies, "I don't know." It is questionable whether such a young child could consent to this work, despite the fact that she had been on camera throughout the prior four seasons of the show as a very small child, highlighting the grey legal and ethical area of child labour when enrolled in parents' work on reality television, and when a child's home has also been turned into a workplace (season 5, episode 2 [Matsumoto 2017]; K. Ryan 2022).

In addition to performances of motherhood with her own children, Chip and Joanna invite their clients to their farm and often spend time with the clients' children, showing them newly born farm animals like goats or chicks, for example. As with Kortney Wilson in *Making It Home*, Joanna is seen playing with her children and those of clients and creating surprises for them. This ritual, repeated through many episodes, reinforces the blurring between home and work for Joanna and Chip and enrols their children in the family-friendly branding of the show as a key element of Joanna Gaines's larger brand. But while bucolic scenes of children frolicking with baby animals helps constitute the brand, the actual work of reproductive labour is gestured towards but largely absent while the children are offscreen. Babysitters or daycare workers are referenced but not seen. Children are present to reproduce the ethos of the show in very specific ways but disappear when their presence is no longer conducive to it.

The frequent appearance of the Gaines children throughout all five seasons of *Fixer Upper* illustrates that the Gaineses can do it all. They just need to be adaptable within the market and, in Joanna's case, work around family life. However, most mothers with a newborn or small children likely would not be able to conduct themselves in the workplace in Joanna Gaines's manner. For example, her employees likely do not bring their newborns to meetings, and their children are probably not seen running around construction sites. Moreover, Joanna's refrain, that she is stretched too thin but she loves it, valorizes an unacceptable work burden for other mothers who work in paid labour. This kind of flexible relationship to labour, largely inaccessible to most workers, does not insist on the proper structural supports but suggests that mothers should be able to balance paid and unpaid labour through their own ingenuity.

The Fallacies of Post-Feminism

Because of the difficulty and exploitation of current labour conditions, we believe depictions of motherhood seen on home design and renovation shows are empowering. They do, after all, challenge some gender roles: Kortney Wilson and Joanna Gaines are, to some degree, in charge. They are the stars of their respective series; they have authority over their employees and apparently also seamlessly manage their children and households, and the shows clearly demonstrate that their husbands adore them.[7] All of this fits the post-feminist logic of achieving entrepreneurial success by savvily working within and reproducing a neoliberal system, even though that system exploits the vast majority of people who operate within it.

By conflating the paid and unpaid labour of motherhood as part of a narrative of hustle, as with all flexible labour, post-feminism expands labour into every corner of our lives. As part of this logic, because this work is thought to be flexible and a matter of choice (e.g., whether a woman runs her own company or works from home), women should be able to fold their unpaid work burden into it. However, reproductive labour is already undervalued and underpaid when paid at all. Moreover, stability in paid labour becomes more scarce as workers participate in flexible labour. Making the labour of mothering superficially visible by performing it in such a cursory and commodified way, while at the same time concealing the actual labour of childcare, makes already invisible labour seem easy, manageable, and completely compatible with market demand. The post-feminist fallacy is that paid labour is the key to liberation for mothers, but there are no reasonable means to it. Therefore, entrepreneurial mothers create their own opportunities, and then their archetype proliferates intertextually, nationally, and internationally to the widest audience possible with the help of private/public partnerships and cultural policies. Yet this cursory modelling of motherwork as part of a mostly white, middle-class moral economy disappears the actual labour of mothering. As discussed further in the next chapter, while good post-feminist mothers are supposedly able to resolve their troubles through choice and self-responsibility, the entrepreneurial tendencies of more problematic mother figures lead to their construction as "bad mothers" on social media.

chapter four

Good Karen, Bad Karen: Visual Culture and the Anti-Vaxx Mom on Reddit

MIRANDA J. BRADY, ERIKA CHRISTIANSEN, AND EMILY HILTZ

In the early decades of the twentieth century, vaccine sceptic and "health entrepreneur" Lora Cornelia Little encouraged citizens to "be your own doctor" by using homeopathic remedies rather than receiving smallpox vaccines (Tolley 2019, 184, citing Little 1913). Little was just one of many maternal figures in anti-inoculation resistance movements who acted as a nurturing counterpoint to masculine doctors and state authorities (Lau 2016; Watling 2019; Durbach 2005). A century later, a similar kind of maternal vaccine skeptic and entrepreneurial spirit would emerge in response to vaccination anxieties and autism.

Like their predecessors, these "mother warriors" assumed the self-appointed role of moral guardians against apparent government and medical science collusion. And while they were significant conspiracy theory propagators, anti-vaccine moms were only one part of a growing scepticism that led the World Health Organization (WHO) to prioritize vaccine hesitancy as a problem demanding global attention in 2019. Even prior to the start of COVID-19, the WHO expressed concern that vaccine scepticism had led to the re-emergence of preventable communicable diseases (Majumder et al. 2015; Patel et al. 2019).

In the United States and Canada, vaccine scepticism occurs in diverse populations – from white libertarians to people of colour, from new immigrant populations to people who have lived in North America for generations – and stronger levels are linked to a distrust of authorities (W. King 2021; Nguyen at al. 2021). Yet, despite the complex picture around vaccination, mother figures often take centre stage as subjects of praise or ridicule in the symbolic terrain.[1] This tension has led to a struggle between anti-vaccine (anti-vaxx) and pro-vaccine (pro-vaxx) sentiment through visual and discursive practices online.

This chapter explores responses to vaccine scepticism in online visual culture through a focus on pre-COVID-19 memes emerging after the millennial turn on Reddit, a social news website and content aggregator, which grew in popularity during the same time period as increasing vaccine scepticism in the early decades of the twenty-first century (Panek 2022).[2] Through visual discourse analysis of memes, we explore the emergence of the pejorative anti-vaxx mom and her conflation with the Karen figure as a response to the mother warrior figure. The mother warrior emerged out of a conservative libertarian conspiracy theory that positioned the good mother as one who resisted vaccinating her child, given vaccines' supposed link to autism. Pro-vaxxers subverted that figure to shame mothers who took the health of their children into their own hands, mocking the anti-vaxx mom and her counterpart, the Karen figure, an entitled and annoying white woman. Both the Karen figure and the anti-vaxx mom figure proliferated with a growing participatory visual culture online (Wiggins 2019; Motrescu-Mayes and Aasman 2019). While anti-vaxx mom and anti-vaxx Karen memes may be humorous and visually effective, they, like the mother warrior figure, reproduce long-entrenched tropes of mother valour and mother blame (or good mother/bad mother) that both attribute broad social problems to mothers and make them responsible for their solutions (Ladd-Taylor and Umansky 1998; Blum 2007; Rich 1976; Thurer 1995). At the root of this struggle are larger questions around world view in which mother figures are deployed in moralistic terms in issues related to population health (Hays 1996; Blum 2007).

A note on terminology: there is a spectrum of perspectives associated with vaccine scepticism, from outright rejection or resistance to vaccine hesitancy and/or delayed inoculation (World Health Organization 2019). Anti-vaxxers, the pejorative catch-all term for people who oppose vaccination (Capurro et al. 2018), is the most prominent term used in pro-vaccination discourses circulating online, and we sometimes employ this term interchangeably with "anti-vaccine" for brevity.

Questioning Authoritative Knowledge through the Mother Warrior

Despite compelling reasons for people to vaccinate themselves and their children, and scientific evidence that modern vaccines are rarely harmful, a minority of the population is vaccine hesitant, while others are vehemently opposed. In addition to safeguarding medical systems from becoming overwhelmed with potential outbreaks, widespread vaccinations are important for vulnerable populations such as older people, infants, and those with autoimmune conditions. In the United States, 1–3 per cent of individuals cannot receive standard vaccinations for health reasons (Stein 2017) and must rely on herd immunity (or sufficient population resistance to diseases).

While having a lot in common with historical examples, contemporary critiques of vaccines emerged in the 1990s along with a shift towards neoliberal models of choice and self-responsibility in healthcare (Jack 2014). Anti-vaccine conspiracy theories gained traction in 1998, when an article by a former doctor, Andrew Wakefield, was published in a medical journal, claiming a direct causal link between vaccinations and autism (Caulfield, Macron, and Murdoch 2017; Fisher and Coulter 2002), a form of social and neurological difference (D. Milton 2020).[3] Wakefield's article was retracted, but controversy over it spurred rumours of a sophisticated cover-up (Caulfield, Macron, and Murdoch 2017), which was reinforced by high-profile vaccination sceptics such as celebrity Jenny McCarthy (Jack 2014; McGuire 2016).

McCarthy's book, *Mother Warriors: A Nation of Parents Healing Autism against All Odds* (2008), in which she attributed her son's autism to vaccinations, helped popularize a specific use of the term "mother warrior." McCarthy, who began her career in the 1990s as a *Playboy* model and irreverent MTV gameshow host, gained a following as the entrepreneur of an autism parent self-help franchise (ABC 2012). By linking autism to external forces, anti-vaccine mothers like McCarthy rejected the mother blame espoused by mid-century behaviourists, who attributed autism to the cold parenting style of mothers (Sousa 2011). At the same time, they turned previous ideas of population health and expertise on their head, claiming vaccines, full of unhealthy, mysterious, and harmful substances, were to blame. This brand of motherhood fuelled distrust in health authorities. Like Lora Little, McCarthy's brand of mother warriors espoused white, conservative sentiment rejecting state overreach into children's welfare; McCarthy herself embodied the archtype as a white, feminine blonde mother from a working-class background (Jack 2014).

Numerous studies, including nine funded or conducted by the US Centers for Disease Control and Prevention, have found no increased risk of autism with vaccinations, even in cases where children were more likely to be autistic (Hviid et al. 2019; Centers for Disease Control and Prevention 2020). Regardless, vaccine scepticism had entered into the online attention economy (Draper 2019; Hills 2019; Wong 2019a and b) where "the most valuable resource in the information era is not information but the attention people pay to it" (Shifman 2013, 32). Movement towards questioning authoritative knowledge while favouring choice and self-responsibility when it came to matters of health has grown exponentially with Web 2.0 and the proliferation of visual participatory culture online (Kata 2012).

Memes, Digital Culture, and Reddit

Among the many powerful visual media that resonate in today's attention economy, memes are particularly potent because they encourage quick and impactful symbolic exchanges and active participation by insiders who understand and propagate popular cultural references (Tufekci 2013). Richard Dawkins ([1976] 1989) first defined the meme as "a [small] unit of cultural transmission, or a unit of imitation" analogous to genes that replicate and mutate (as cited in Shifman 2013, 340). Wiggins (elaborates further, defining internet memes more specifically as "a remixed, iterated message that can be rapidly diffused by members of participatory digital culture for the purpose of satire, parody, critique, or other discursive activity" (2019, 11).

Internet memes are generated by "networked publics" and have the power to "affect national conversations and online spectacles" (Tufekci 2013, 849). Many are image macros, multimodal combinations of photographic images and boldface text, and they can take various forms, such as an image, short video, or GIF (looped animation). With the proliferation of digital technologies, many people are able to create memes, making them an accessible form of participatory culture (Wiggins 2019).

Beyond their multimodality, memes are most appealing when their elements are open to interpretation and creative action, enticing users' participation through imitation and remix (Shifman 2013; Segev et al. 2015) as well as when communities have the ability to "fill in necessary or absent information" based on their intertextual and specialized group knowledge (Wiggins 2019, 6). The more a meme circulates and adapts, the more recognizable it becomes.

Memes are circulated and take on new connotations via online sites like Reddit, one of the most popular social media and content aggregate platforms, with 330 million active users per month and 21 billion screenviews (Foundation 2021). Reddit began in 2005 and evolved with search engines and user-generated content online, with the latter quickly outnumbering earlier kinds of posts such as links to mainstream news stories (Panek 2022). By 2006, site administrators created "subreddits" to organize site content thematically. The platform saw a boom in 2008–9, and, eventually, more than a million subreddits had developed, some with millions of users each (Panek 2022, 3). Posts are ranked by algorithms that prioritize those with the rate and number of user upvotes, a form of user affirmation unique to Reddit (Panek 2022).

As Panek points out, Reddit's model circumvented traditional news gatekeeping, with some seeing the platform as more "democratic" and "authentic" (2022, 23). Panek draws the connection between this particular understanding of the site and increasingly vitriolic political posts on social media, culminating in the 2016 US presidential election, in which Donald Trump challenged mainstream news and authoritative knowledge. Memes posted by vaccine sceptics spread widely over Reddit in the first decades of the twenty-first century, often featuring questionable doctors or frightening-looking syringes pointed at babies. These were countered with pro-vaccination memes, which employed their own visual arguments, often featuring the anti-vaxx mom, including the anti-vaxx mom as Karen figure.

Karen's Emergence in Online Visual Culture

The exact origin of the Karen figure is debated (Nagesh 2020). However, it has increasingly come to signify an entitled, irritating white woman. Know Your Meme credits the film *Mean Girls* as one of the first places "Karen" appeared, citing the line "Oh my God, Karen, you can't just ask someone why they're white," which is directed at the character Karen Smith (Waters 2004). The film is a modern-day cult classic, spawning thousands of parodies, tributes, and memes. Karen (played by Amanda Seyfried) is depicted as a popular, blonde, unintelligent high school mean girl.

In a Tumblr post from 20 October 2016, a Karen figure appeared in a parody of a Nintendo advertisement in which a woman brings her Nintendo Switch to a party. The post jokes, "Oh shit, Karen brought her stupid Nintendo thing to the party again. We're DRINKING, Karen. We're having CONVERSATIONS." While the original ad did not use the name Karen, the caption of the macro image contributed to an emerging online vocabulary about Karens.

On 7 December 2017 the Reddit subreddit r/fuckyoukaren was created, based on posts of a user by the name /u/fuck_you_karen (account since deleted). The user's name pertained to his online persona (whether real or fabricated) and his hatred for his ex-wife, named Karen, who apparently took custody of their kids in a divorce. After the original user account was deleted, the "fuckyoukaren" subreddit was created as a hub for all posts related to the Karen figure (Romano 2020). Later that month, on 25 December, a Reddit user claiming to be named Karen created a post in which she asked why she was receiving messages from her friends telling her to "fuck off." Users pointed out the rising popularity of the Karen meme and the posts made by /u/fuck_you_karen. As a result, the subreddit eventually made a permanent post on the front page: "Please don't harass innocent Karens." Feeding back into the Karen stereotype, the post states that harassing innocent Karens makes a person no better than the original Karen herself, further solidifying the archetype.

Panek describes the r/fuckyoukaren subreddit as an example of a "spectacle subreddit," where virtual communities collectively pass "moral judgment" on and express outrage at bad behaviour gone unpunished (2022, 17). The potent annoyance, judgment, and humour directed at the Karen figure continued to grow in the years following its emergence. During analysis for this chapter in 2019, the subreddit had 190,000 followers. As of May 2021, it had grown to 1.8 million, indicating wide user interest in Karen content.

Karen has acquired additional characteristics and notoriety through memes. For instance, she's present in the "I'd like to speak to your manager" meme, in "she took the fucking kids" subreddits, and in pro-vaccination memes that poke fun at anti-vaxxers via Karen. An entry in the Urban Dictionary describes Karen as a "mother of three. blond. owns a volvo. annoying as hell. wears acrylics 24/7. currently at your workplace speaking to your manager" (Kolodiejzyk 2018). In 2020, Karen became a popular figure in anti-racism discourses following the death of George Floyd. During this time, the Karen moniker was increasingly used online to critique arrogant white women as well as racism and white supremacy (A. Williams 2020). Karen was easily signified vis-à-vis internet memes on Reddit, and this also led to her cultural resonance, with the anti-vaxx mom being one iteration.

Identifying Pattens in Participatory Visual Culture

The memes described in this chapter were singular, static still images that multiplied through varied mutations online leading up to the summer of 2019, when we conducted our research. While there are a number of visual patterns in pro- and anti-vaccination sentiment online, repeated in the former were anti-vaxx mom and anti-vaxx mom as Karen memes, which included digital photographs from films, television episodes, or stock images with pithy captions.

Such meme images are constitutive of broader sentiments or discourse about inoculation, good and bad mothering, and authoritative knowledge (Wiggins 2019). Like other discourses, they are part of a system of knowledge reproduced across cultural sites, which makes some possibilities available while delimiting or foreclosing others (Foucault 1972). Moreover, memes do not solely comprise surface elements, but reproduce cultural values and a host of visual actions and relations (Sturken and Cartwright 2009, 25). They also employ rapid modes of signification and highly impactful uses of sign systems (Barthes 1972; Baudrillard 1983).

In critically examining memes as elements of visual discourse, it is important to consider composition, including remix and intertextuality, as well as characteristic amateur aesthetics (Motrescu-Mayes and Aasman 2019; Wiggins 2019). For example, the addition of the signature Karen hair in some memes can look tacked on like a bad wig, adding a humorous element. Considering a "horizon of historic events" (Christmann 2008, para. 1) as well as audience reception are other important points of contextualization. Though images are polysemic and may have many different readings, depending on the subject position of those decoding them, dominant readings of memes, or those interpretations encouraged by their encoders through the use of particular forms of signification (Hall [1973] 1991), may be enabled in several ways. For example, overlaid text, captions, the names of posts, upvotes, threads, and subreddits all help to inform an understanding of image meanings. A base knowledge of a discursive formation, popular culture, and symbolic exchange are also necessary for interpretation, and this may be somewhat specialized within particular subreddit participant groups, as there are specific norms and affordances with any platform, including Reddit.

Sentiment can be read through repeated visual and textual elements (Gries 2015) manifested across memes. In anti-vaccination and pro-vaccination memes, women, and mothers in particular, are routinely the focal point of vaccination debates, whether overt or implicit. In some cases, mothers are referenced but not directly pictured or named – for example, through use of a mother's apparent voice or an analogy or when a mother is the party to which a comment is directed.

In the next section, we discuss examples of pro-vaxx memes about anti-vaxxers that overwhelmingly feature anti-vaxx moms and the exasperating Karen archetype as an anti-vaxx mom. These archetypes appeared in a total of 112 memes, which we found through the following keyword searches on Reddit in the summer of 2019: anti vax karen, anti vaxx karen, anti vax mom, anti vaccine karen, anti shot karen, anti immunization karen.

We acknowledge that many visitors to Reddit and other social media sites may see but not vote or comment on content (Panek 2022). Yet, popular patterns may be identified through a focus on large numbers of upvotes as one indicator of resonance with users. Therefore, we generally discuss those memes with more than a thousand upvotes. There are a few exceptions: we elected to include three images with less than one thousand upvotes because they explicitly mentioned Karen or exemplified a broader senti-ment – that is, the misguided nature of the white, anti-vaxx mother who threatens the life of her children and broader population.

Use of the words "Karen" and "mom" were repeated, as were images of feminine-presenting subjects positioned as mothers (they were often seen alongside children or named "mom" in cap-tions or comments). While one might expect the presence of two or more parents in a discourse so heavily tied to children's health, fathers are comparatively absent (Spencer 2019). Notable here is the construction of Karen as a white, cisgender, heterosexual woman; absent are diverse representations such as LGBTQ+ portrayals.[4] Thus, her entitled persona is interrelated with her cisgender and (assumed) heterosexual identity, along with her whiteness.

Anti-Vaxx Moms, Karen, and the Domestic Sphere of "Research"

In both anti-vaccine and pro-vaccine memes, women are consis-tently featured in domestic scenes as enterprising white mothers highly concerned with their children's welfare. Pro-vaxx memes, however, openly mock anti-vaxx mothers' enterprising spirit as imperilling their own children and society at large. While the anti-vaxx mom displayed in upvoted Reddit memes seems the binary opposite of the sentiment of the empowered mother warrior, both embody neoliberal and post-feminist sentiments of choice and consumption (Kennedy 2017; Vandenbeld Giles 2014a).

The main source of enterprise for anti-vaxx moms in pro-vaxx memes is in conducting their own research on vaccines in domestic settings. Such an initiative is mocked in a popular meme featuring a woman in a white lab coat, wearing gloves and goggles, and working with test tubes (thus coded as a scientist), with the textual overlay "Vaccine Research," juxtaposed with an image of a woman sitting on a toilet, shorts down, looking at her cellphone, with the caption "Anti Vax Mom Research." Although no children are featured in the second image, the textual overlay indicates it is of a mother who is a vaccine sceptic. This use of juxtaposition and humour indicates the lack of validity of vaccine-sceptic information. The meme clearly expresses pro-vaxx sentiment: the white anti-vaxx mom's research takes place casually on a toilet on her mobile phone, rather than in a lab with scientific equipment.

Another meme with over 12,000 upvotes similarly criticizes a young blonde "worried mom" who "does better research than the FBI." While she is not conducting her anti-vaccination research on the toilet, the meme repeats the domestic situating of a young mother doing her own investigations at home. The quotation marks around "researcher" reflect a repeated theme across pro-vaxx memes, marking women's anti-vaxx research as questionable. Poking fun at anti-vaxxer mistrust of government agencies and the shift toward distrust of health authorities, the meme suggests that this mom believes her investigations are more legitimate than "official"' research.

The theme of domesticity continues in another upvoted meme (8.2 thousand upvotes), titled "When Karen doesn't leave." In it, a family sits around the table while a girl asks her male and female coded parents, "Why don't we get vaccines?" The dad – one of a few father figures in the sample – responds as he smiles at his daughter: "Honey why would we trust doctors when we can trust the internet?" Like the repeated placement of anti-vaxx mothers

Figure 4.1. A meme image comparing "vaccine research" in a lab environment to "anti vax mom research" occurring in a washroom. Upper image: iStock.com/anyaivanova

in domestic spaces, this meme depicts a stock image of a seemingly happy young white family at home that sees the internet as a trusted source of knowledge. However, the children's responses – "I miss my brother" and "My blood hurts" – darkly contrast with the saccharine image of the perfect white kitchen with well-stocked fruit bowl in the foreground.

In other memes, references to essential oils similarly depict anti-vaxx mothers as illogical non-scientists who trust "at home" remedies over scientifically proven vaccines. One meme with over a thousand upvotes depicts a child-parent conversation in which the child asks their mom if they can get vaccinated, only for the mother to respond, "No. We already have vaccines at home." A stock image of syringes and vials of vaccinations is juxtaposed with honey, ginger, garlic, essential oils, and citrus fruits – apparently this mom's homeopathic version of vaccinations. When essential oils and other natural remedies appear in such pro-vaxx memes about anti-vaxxers, mothers in particular are critiqued. Moreover, the consistent reference to natural remedies functions to connect domestication with anti-vaxx mothers in a space of non- and pseudo-science.

The inclusion of children in pro-vaxx memes serves to emphasize anti-vaxx hypocrisy – mothers being overly concerned about their children's welfare while inadvertently endangering their children. For instance, a meme featuring a still from *Spider-Man* (2002) shows a large-statured male wrestler holding up three fingers, contextualized through the caption, "Anti-vax moms to their newborn child after denying vaccines: I've got you for three minutes."

Similarly, another meme uses a smirking image of Jim, a character from the American television show *The Office* (2005–13), watching from behind window blinds to mimic the looming threat of polio for an unvaccinated child. Displayed in text below the image, the unseen anti-vaxx mom states, "Omg [oh my God] our children are so healthy as they don't have any vaccine poisons in them." Anti-vaxxers consistently blame these "poisons" for children's autism, which is treated by anti-vaxxers as worse than measles and death. Another meme in our sample pokes fun at this sentiment: in a post titled "Death > autism," a person holds their hands in prayer and closes their eyes (as though thanking the Lord) as the caption reads, "anti-vax parents when their kid dies from measles instead of being diagnosed as autistic."

One of the highest-rated/upvoted posts within the Reddit sample also pokes fun at the anti-vaxx mom's hypocritical concern with internet safety, with the text "install[ing] anti-virus on your computer but not on you [the child]" (figure 4.2). A blonde woman with a neat ponytail is centred in the first image, and her intense smiling expression is directed down towards an unseen child. The image on the right is an unsettling extreme close-up of her eyes. The woman depicted in this meme also appears in a carpet cleaner advertisement and is part of a meme collection labelled "The What" (The What / Rug Doctor Woman ad). The humour of this ad arises both from this image as nostalgic stock art meant to connote a wholesome clean home and its unsettling recontextualization, which again troubles the domestic realm. The cropping of the original image, which highlights her pleasant but unnerving gaze, encourages viewers to assess the woman's look alongside the anti-vaxx mom's exasperating hypocrisy.

When your anti-vax mom installs anti-virus on your computer but not on you

Figure 4.2. This Reddit meme entitled "I'm anti-anti-vax moms" is captioned, "When your anti-vax mom installs anti-virus on your computer but not on you." The two images, one of a smiling blonde, white woman and the other an extreme close-up of the same woman's eyes and intense gaze, suggest this mother figure's unsettling and perhaps sinister intentions.

Keeping children safe from vaccine injury by exposing them to harmful diseases is understood in the pro-vaxx memes as a hypocritical form of parental child endangerment. One meme with more than thirty-three thousand upvotes pokes fun at this failure in logic and anti-vaxx mothers' perceived unintelligence and willful ignorance; in the meme, a *Futurama* (1999–2013) cartoon character states, "I don't understand vaccines and I have to protect my kids from understanding it. We will not give in to the thinkers." Other upvoted memes on Reddit display teens getting vaccinated despite their anti-vaxx moms' efforts, sometimes with the help of their fathers.[5] Within this theme, there is a sub-narrative of fathers secretly vaccinating their children and tricking anti-vaxx moms.

The presentation of mothers as unintelligent and easily duped, with skewed priorities, was a key theme. For example, one meme reads, "When your mom catches you vaccinating yourself, but you say you were just doing heroin." The caption indicates not only that the mother figure is easy to trick, but also that she is so unreasonable as to think vaccines are worse than heroin.

Other memes demonstrate anti-vaxx mothers as diabolical and often play on themes of mothers wishing to harm their children. A meme featuring a still of Larry the Lobster from *SpongeBob SquarePants* (1999–present) implies anti-vaxxers are attempting a sneaky "trick" to end the life of an undesired child. Titled "Anti-Vaxers," the caption reads, "You can't abort a child after they have been born."

While all of these memes use varied incongruencies between captioned text and associated image to produce humour, the anti-vaxx mom appears with remarkable memetic consistency through the image of Karen. Within our Reddit sample, the visual and thematic markers for Karen circulate with consistency as a haughty and annoying white mother. In pro-vaxx memes, one of the key markers for Karen's white motherhood is her haircut – usually a bottle-blonde "mom" hairstyle with chunky highlights, shorter, voluminous hair in the back with a longer, sleek front, sometimes with a side-swept bang. In some memes, the hairstyle is digitally imposed on fictional, masculinized characters to signal their likeness to Karen, such as Thanos from the Marvel saga (2008–19), who, renamed Karenos, collects infinity oils to "save her anti vaxx kid." Another meme places the haircut on an adapted Borg character from *Star Trek: Voyager* (1995–2001): here, Karen of Borg, part of the "Anti-Vaxx Collective," is shown inquiring about the vessel manager.

A series of pro-vaxx memes featuring anti-vaxx Karen were produced out of screenshots of a Sims 4 Karen figure, also with short blonde hair. A Reddit user posted Sims 4 Karen images of the figure's imagined home. In the house tour images, Karen, who is identified as "anti-vax," has started an (apparently unsuccessful) business out of her home selling essential oils, and she is sarcastically described as thinking of herself as a "brave #BossBabe and #Mom." References to alcohol in this series imply that Karen is masking a drinking problem: she has "a 'decorative' bottle of scotch," and the kitchen features "more sparse alcohol bottles 'for cooking.'" Poking fun at Karen's #BossBabe image, the user's caption explains that "we see some jewelry and crystals Karen tried to sell online. She has more of that merchandise in storage 'cus, despite her salesma'amship, hardly anyone wants her shit." This reference to the entrepreneurial mom again ties the anti-vaxxer to domestic spaces, where she presents herself as a legitimate health expert. Here, the sentiment expressed is similar to that of other memes in the sample. Anti-vaxx Karen epitomizes the "bad" mother figure, whose actions are abhorrent, or at least extremely misguided, as they run counter to mothers' apparently natural maternal characteristics (Blum 2007). As with other memes, this positions the mother as the self-absorbed obstacle to children's safety and society more broadly.

Meme Mothers as Trouble

The emergence of participatory visual culture (Wiggins 2019) and platforms like Reddit enabled the proliferation of anti-vaccination sentiment and the rejection of authority by circumventing traditional media gatekeepers (Milner 2013). The enterprising mother warrior figure was one antidote to the perceived over-reach of state and private interests. On the other hand, pro-vaxxers use the same platforms and techniques to respond with their own visual arguments: anti-vaxx mom and anti-vaxx mom as Karen memes equate anti-vaccination sentiment with white, irksome, entitled, misguided, and even diabolical bad mothers. These memes, which use humour and remixing, are generally very effective in conveying their message because they reproduce broader discursive formations and have a receptive audience who understand what they signify. Hence their popularity indicated by upvoting.

While pro- and anti-vaccine sentiment in visual culture may indicate vastly different ideological orientations, our analysis of popular upvoted pro-vaxx Reddit memes highlights their digital proximity and discursive connections. Anti-vaxx moms and mother warriors are part of the same continuum of good/bad motherhood and the assumption that women should be a natural source of care for children and larger population health (Blum

2007), an assumption that allows widespread struggles over vaccination to be placed on their shoulders. As early historical examples of inoculation discourse illustrate (Durbach 2005), the mother is a central motif used to communicate anxieties about the state's encroachment into domestic, private matters, which extended with the figure of the mother warrior. However, by subverting the good mother into the bad mother, Karen and other anti-vaxx mom figures reproduce the same mother valour / mother blame binary (Blum 2007; Caplan 2010; Ladd-Taylor and Umansky 1998). By extension, then, mothers are held responsible for broader sociocultural and political problems – in this case, the proliferation of vaccine hesitancy, which has spread globally and across diverse demographics, not just among white libertarian women (World Health Organization 2019). A reductive and moralistic focus on so-called anti-vaxx moms limits our view of this problem and does little to solve it.

This leads us to ask, is mother blame really the best approach for debunking the flawed logics of anti-vaxxers? We hope there will be more effective pro-vaccination appeals, as the moral condemnation of vaccine scepticism vis-à-vis mother figures has been unconvincing for the portion of the population that has lost trust in health authorities.

Disappearing Mom: Maternal Estrangement and Televisual Alienation in *Modern Family* and *Shameless*

Family estrangement is fairly common, with one in four Americans reporting estrangement from one or more family members (Pillemer 2020). Yet there are few constructive models of family estrangement in popular culture, including maternal estrangement, which can be particularly difficult (Schoppe-Sullivan et al. 2021). Underlying this paucity of social acknowledgment is the assumption that families are an intact, atomized unit (Scharp and Hall 2017), and a sense of stigma when this is not the case (Agllias 2013). This is despite the shifting expectations around family roles and composition over the past several decades following second wave feminism, including increases in divorce or separation and lone-parent households (OECD 2011). The examples of estrangement that do exist often depict a resolution where family members set aside their differences and reunite after a conflict.[1] The reality, however, is that family estrangements are often painful and continuous for many people (Agllias 2013; Blake et al. 2020; Boss1999).

This chapter explores instances of white-coded maternal physical and emotional estrangement in two popular shows that were streaming in the United States and Canada after the start of COVID-19 through the online platform Netflix. During this period, many people were watching television shows as a way to offset the loneliness of social isolation, which was likely compounded for those with family difficulties (Blake et al. 2020).[2] In this chapter, I compare the largely absent mothers DeDe Pritchett and Monica Gallagher in the shows *Modern Family* and *Shameless*, respectively, who are both blamed for their estrangements from their families due to their own poor choices. In these shows, bad mothers opt out of mothering, or do not perform it well in the limited time when they do appear. Both shows employ the trope of mother blame (Blum 2007; Ladd-Taylor and Umansky 1998) to alienate audiences from missing mother figures through a process I call televisual alienation. "Televisual alienation" can be understood as the process whereby a television show disappears the mother figure from the audience so that most of our knowledge of her is through the disparaging accounts of the main characters, and her actual appearances are extreme and fraught.

Modern Family is a family-friendly show that first aired on ABC in 2009; *Shameless*, which began airing on Showtime in 2011, was much more adult oriented and included nudity, cursing, and illegal drug use. Yet, despite these differences, the shows treat maternal estrangement in similar ways, using the same techniques of maternal "absent presence."[3] While both shows focus on white-coded families, the former centres on an upper-middle class family, and the latter on a family of a lower socio-economic status. The transcendence of mother blame across these shows and class depictions as an explanation for white maternal absence illustrates the cultural resonance of this trope. While the absent mother narrative has a long history (Astrom 2017),[4] this chapter illustrates contemporary televisual variations that allow for the juxtaposition of good and bad mothers.

Though largely absent, the characters DeDe Pritchett in *Modern Family* and Monica Gallagher in *Shameless* act as vehicles for the premises of both shows and for the development of the main cast of characters. In both shows, the death of these mothers (who were already ancillary characters) was used as a plot device to create drama for the main characters without removing anyone central to the show. In both cases, these mothers caused more havoc in their presence than in death, indicating that the families – that is, the compilation of main characters – were better-off without them.

Both *Modern Family* and *Shameless* illustrate examples of maternal physical and emotional estrangement. As Agllias explains, "physical estrangement is when one or more family members cease all contact," whereas "emotional estrangement is when family members maintain some perfunctory contact that is characterized by infrequency, discomfort, and dissatisfaction" (2013, 309). Similarly, Schoppe-Sullivan et al. note that estrangement refers to "an increase in distancing toward discontinuation of the relationship initiated by at least one party in response to their perception of a negative or damaged relationship" and can be both "geographical" and "psychological," which, especially in the latter case, may mean there is still limited but strained contact (2021, para. 3). The examples explored in this chapter include physical estrangement, when one character has lost or chosen not to be in contact with another family member or members, and emotional or psychological estrangement, where family members have lapses in contact with their mothers or are in touch with them infrequently, and their relationship is tense.

Estrangement and Alienation

There are a number of reasons for family estrangement, including interpersonal dynamics, divorce or separation, alienation, marginalization, abuse, addiction, trauma, differences in political orientation, generational divides, perceived betrayal, challenges to cultural belief systems, economic struggle or other stressors, and unmet expectations (Agllias 2013; Schoppe-Sullivan et al. 2021; Scharp and Hall 2017). In addition to these are many other possible explanations for involuntary maternal absence. These may include a lack of financial means and/or parenting skills, incarceration, and intergenerational trauma, which, in Canada, are experienced disproportionately by Indigenous women, due to the legacies of colonization, residential schools, and the 60s Scoop (Truth and Reconciliation Commission 2015; National Inquiry 2019; Major 2021; Greenslade 2017). Another potential reason for maternal absence is participation in global labour flows (Tong 2007; Duffy 2007; Henaway 2023).

Family estrangements can be inherited or can result from first-hand experience (Agllias 2013). While seeking distance from problematic relationships can, in many cases, be beneficial (Scharp and Hall 2017), it is also often accompanied by "disenfranchised grief" (Agllias 2011) – that is, a lack of social acknowledgment, with few outlets demonstrating how to mourn the loss of a family member who is still living but psychologically absent. As Pauline Boss notes, such an "ambiguous loss" can be "the most distressful of all losses," due to its continuing uncertainty (1999, 6). Family estrangements can also result in economic precarity as well as a loss of networks of social support (Blake et al. 2020).

Estrangement is more likely to be initiated by adult children than parents (Schoppe-Sullivan et al. 2021), and parents who are estranged from adult children report the experience as a traumatic and devastating loss that is coupled with uncertainty and social stigma (Agllias 2013; Schoppe-Sullivan et al. 2021). Adult children tend to have closer relationships with mothers than with fathers, and therefore "greater relational distress and tension may exist between estranged mothers and children, which may exert a stronger adverse impact on their well-being" (Schoppe-Sullivan et al. 2021, para. 4).

While adult children may feel at liberty to opt out of family relationships that they see as "nonvoluntary" (Scharp and Hall 2017, 28), older generations of mothers, following social expectations of earlier eras, frequently feel their identities are tightly bound to motherhood, especially where they do not have other social outlets (Agllias 2013). Shoppe-Sullivan et al. (2021) report that mothers of estranged children frequently attribute the estrangement to external rather than internal factors, indicating, for example, that a spouse of a child or another parent had turned their child against them. The latter phenomenon, known as "child alienation," has been referenced in legal scholarship in cases involving custody battles, though these generally relate to children who are minors (Drozd and Olesen 2004). Kelly and Johnston suggest that child alienation includes "unreasonable negative feelings ... toward a parent that are significantly disproportionate to the child's actual experience with that parent" (2001, 251). They note the importance of distinguishing alienated children who reject one parent as a result of the influence of a "programming" parent from those who reject parents due to a myriad of other factors (251). As I argue below, we can take concepts like child alienation and adapt them to better understand broader familial dynamics between adult children and parents (rather than just minors) and the techniques and discourses employed to portray and extend their effects onscreen.

Mother Blame and Mothers Behaving Badly

As discussed in previous chapters, Western motherhood is an institution that follows a long history bound up with ideas related to morality, placing the obligations of social reproduction on women through cultural, familial, and economic pressures (Rich1976; James [1952] 2012; Barrett and McIntosh 1982; Federici 2004, 2020). These pressures work to bind women's identities to motherhood as natural, although it is a highly contextual construct (Blum 2007). Following long-standing patterns of gender-, race-, and class-inflected binaries in discourse and popular culture related to so-called good and bad mothers (Collins 1990; Story 2014), mother blame is a trope that shares a long history with motherhood. According to Linda Blum, "the mother-valor/mother-blame binary serves, in modern Western cultures, to hold mothers responsible for child outcomes and thus for the health of families, future citizens, and the nation. Such good mothers, with ostensibly selfless devotion, are policed and police themselves through fear of mother-blame, being judged as inadequate, unnatural, or selfish" (2007, 202). Women who do not conform to this gendered standard of nurturing caregiver are often blamed for their children's problems and constituted as bad mothers. Even when mothers do conform, struggles faced by children are frequently attributed to bad mothering. This judgment of mothers is in line with Western pressures related to intensive mothering, where a mother is expected to be selflessly dedicated to the development of her child (Hays 1998). By extension, many mothers who are perceived to fail at nurturing the bond or attachment with their children feel a sense of inadequacy (Agllias 2013), as "caregiving is maintained as 'naturally' gendered and central to normative femininity" (Blum 2007, 202).

Despite the prevalence of binary constructs of motherhood, scholars of post-feminism (Gill 2007; Kennedy 2017) have pointed out new discourses where some forms of questionable maternal behaviour have become more acceptable. Jo Littler (2020) makes a connection between the transmediated discourse of "mothers behaving badly" (MBB) and a neoliberal crisis in social reproduction. MBB are generally young, overworked, white, middle-class mothers who have been driven to the brink with the unreasonable, gendered demands of motherhood. Therefore, their temporary transgressions and shirking of their maternal duties are often depicted as justified, or at least understandable (Littler 2020). But while these transgressions are somewhat inappropriate (drinking, partying, or staying out late), they frequently empower MBB in some way. In the end, these mothers ease back on their hedonistic behaviours while learning the lesson that their boldness will enable them to challenge double standards with men (Littler 2020). At the end of the story, then, these are "good" mothers who were only temporarily "bad."

MBB are not mothers who permanently distance themselves from their maternal roles, as with DeDe in *Modern Family*, or who transgress too much in their partying, unlike Monica in *Shameless*. As discussed below, while DeDe and Monica do indeed behave badly, they are distinct from the MBB, as their choices have resulted in lasting family estrangements that are never really resolved. Rather than merely behaving badly, these are constructs of bad mothers who are to blame for their own poor life choices.

The Missing Mother in *Modern Family*

The scene starts with the ominous music from the impending shark attack in the film *Jaws*, as Alex sits before her cello in her bedroom. In the kitchen, her mother, Claire, has poured herself a glass of white wine, trying to mentally prepare herself for what she knows is coming. The music quickens and intensifies. DeDe has entered the house, and she sneaks up behind her daughter. The analogy of a predator about to pounce is clear, as Claire turns around terrified to see her mother, who immediately begins to berate her. DeDe then mentions that she ran into Claire's long-lost ex-boyfriend from high school, whom she has invited for dinner that night at Claire's house, where Claire now lives with her husband and children. Claire's shocked expression indicates her disapproval of DeDe's invitation. To make matters worse, by the end of the night, DeDe is seen passionately kissing her daughter's ex-boyfriend. As in each of the few episodes in which DeDe appears, she causes a scene and disrupts the loving but at times fragile dynamics of the main characters on *Modern Family*. "Why does everything always have to be so hard with you?" Claire demands later in the same episode, and indeed things are hard whenever DeDe appears and even when she is merely referenced (season 10, episode 5 [Ko 2011]).

The ABC series *Modern Family*, which ran for eleven seasons from 2009 to 2020, is made up of an ensemble cast featuring Jay Pritchett (Ed O'Neill) and his second wife, Gloria Delgado Pritchett (Sofia Vergara), Gloria's son from her first marriage, Manny (Rico Rodriguez), and later their child, Joe (Jeremy Maguire); Jay's daughter Claire (Julie Bowen), her husband, Phil (Ty Burrell), and their three children, Alex (Ariel Winter), Luke (Nolan Gould), and Haley (Sarah Hyland); Jay's son, Mitchell (Jesse Tyler Ferguson), his husband, Cameron (Eric Stonestreet), and their daughter Lily (Aubrey Anderson-Emmons, from season 3). The show largely revolves around the extended family spending time together as well as the three distinct family units in which motherwork is performed by stay-at-home parents Gloria, Cameron, and Claire (none work in paid labour in the first season). DeDe's appearances are infrequent, in only eight episodes out of 250, or about 3 per cent, and DeDe is not featured in any of the signature promotional family portraits created for each season, which feature the main cast members. As Bradley (2018) notes, Jay's French bulldog, Stella, appears in more episodes than DeDe.

Nonetheless, intermittent references to an absent DeDe also indicate that she makes life difficult for the family, especially Claire, with whom she is critical and passive aggressive. While DeDe has a closer relationship with her son, Mitchell, which sometimes involves her using him to manipulate the family (season 1, episode

4 [Levitan 2009]), Claire and DeDe generally spend time together only at family events like weddings (season 7, episode 21 [Pollock and Walls 2016]; season 8, episode 11 [Levitan, Lloyd, and Higginbotham 2017]) and birthday parties (season 2, episode 15 [Ko 2011]), for which DeDe comes to town in the episode referenced previously. DeDe and Claire's contact is "perfunctory" and characterized by "infrequency, discomfort, and dissatisfaction" (Agllias 2013, 309), indicating the emotional estrangement between mother and daughter. DeDe also has particular animosity for Jay's second and much younger wife, Gloria, of whom she is intensely jealous in early seasons of the show. This dynamic is a recurring joke: even when it seems DeDe has turned a corner, she lunges for Gloria at the last minute, trying to choke her (season 1, episode 4 [Levitan 2009]). It is clear that, during the time before the start of season 1, DeDe has been emotionally and physically estranged from most of the family, at least partly due to her inappropriate behaviour at Jay and Gloria's wedding, at which she became heavily intoxicated and caused a scene, as is shown in a flashback (season 1, episode 4 [Levitan 2009]) .

DeDe is clearly portrayed as the one to blame for her antics, though Jay is a rather difficult character who struggles to demonstrate affection for his children. And, while it is alluded to that Jay did very little of the work of reproductive labour, comments related to DeDe's role in child rearing are generally derogatory (e.g., season 4, episode 2 [Zucker and Lloyd 2013]). It was DeDe's decision to leave Jay and her children to explore new life experiences, with her apparent eccentricity reaching its pinnacle sometime in midlife. As she tells Jay sadly, "I just don't want to be thought of as Crazy Nanna" (season 2, episode 15 [Ko 2009]), though the family clearly sees her in this way. Her New Age markers, like vegetarianism, meditation, and homeopathic remedies, are referenced humorously. DeDe's decision to leave seems to make it more palatable to audiences for Jay to have moved on so seamlessly with his much younger and heteronormatively attractive second wife (season 4, episode 2 [Zucker and Lloyd 2013]).

Featured in only eight episodes by season 10, the last of which happens posthumously through a voicemail, DeDe dies (season 10, episode 5 [Chandrasekaran 2018]). Because she is a stock character about whom we know very little, this episode is more about what Claire and Mitchell suffer with their loss than about DeDe herself, which is reinforced through the episode's title, "Good Grief." As show producer Steve Levitan states of the choice, "It occurred to us that death is a giant part of the family experience … We've never seen the entire family have to deal with such a loss" (Bradley 2018, para. 3).

Even in death, DeDe's difficult personality is noted: she died peacefully in her sleep with a smile on her face "clutching a 10-page list of suggestions for hotel staff" (season 10, episode 5 [Chandrasekaran 2018]). The wedge she created between her children also continues to cause conflict. Mitchell mentions to Claire that he was able to tell DeDe "she was a wonderful mother," noting that he was glad that this was the last thing he said to her. Claire, clearly disturbed by this revelation, and the fact that Mitchell always had a better relationship with DeDe, notes that their last interaction was a fight over a social media post where DeDe promoted a homeopathic remedy. Claire can think only of negative memories of her mother – "Remember when mom said I ate ice cream like a prostitute?" and, "I just feel so guilty because sometimes I was as mean to her as she was to me" (season 10, episode 5 [Chandrasekaran 2018]). However, in a later episode in the following season, when DeDe's second husband, Jerry, shows up with some of the items left to the family in DeDe's will, Claire finally manages to think fondly of her mother (season 11, episode 8 [Lloyd, Levitan, and Walls 2020]).

The *Shameless* Mother

Shameless is a Showtime series based on a British series of the same name with its most prominent star, William H. Macy, playing Frank Gallagher, a dysfunctional alcoholic and father of six, whose wife, Monica, has left the family before the show's start. The show ran for eleven seasons with 140 episodes from 2011 to 2021. Like *Modern Family*, *Shameless* has a compilation cast of main characters, including Monica and Frank's children Fiona (Emmy Rossum), Phillip "Lip" (Jeremy Allen White), Ian (Cameron Monaghan), Carl (Ethan Cutkosky), Debbie (Emma Kenney), and the toddler, Liam (Christian Isaiah). Monica's absence and Frank's dysfunction cause major hardship for Fiona, the eldest of the children, who takes on the primary caregiving responsibilities for her siblings when the youngest is just an infant and she herself is still a teenager (pilot [Abbott and Wells 2011]). While Monica is characterized as selfish in her absence, Fiona is depicted as self-sacrificing for performing the motherwork that Monica has left behind. Although Monica (played by Chloe Webb) appears in only thirteen episodes, or less than 10 per cent of the show, she leaves a potent legacy.

Monica is referenced several times in derogatory terms (pilot [Abbott and Wells 2011]) before she first appears in only one episode of season 1, when Frank lures her to their neighborhood by pretending she has won a prize in a contest; this is a ruse to get her to sign insurance settlement paperwork so Frank can collect a monetary claim. Monica's reappearance gives her the opportunity to reunite with the children after nearly two years of her absence with no contact. Despite her attempts at expressing affection, her children reject her. While Monica is visiting, a paternity test reveals that Ian was fathered by Frank's brother. Monica confesses that she does not remember how she became pregnant with Ian, as she was taking a lot of drugs at the time (season 1, episode 10 [Caponera 2011]). She comments later, in season 2, that all of her children were conceived on different substances, indicating her pattern of substance abuse (season 2, episode 9 [Borstein 2012]), and Frank indicates in episode 1 that a doctor had informed him that Carl has fetal alcohol spectrum disorder (FASD), indicating that Monica's substance abuse continued while she was pregnant (season 1, episode 2 [Abbott and Wells 2011]).[5]

At her children's behest, Monica disappears again and does not return until the end of season 2; her children seem to have no contact with her during this time. When Monica reappears, her addiction and apparent bipolar disorder are noted over the arch of four episodes starting with episode 9. When Fiona awakens one morning to find Monica in the kitchen making breakfast, she states,

"We don't have any money," assuming Monica is just there to take advantage of the family (season 2, episode 9 [Borstein 2012]).

Some of the family begins getting more used to having Monica back, as she tries to win their trust, but it is clear that the dynamic she has with Frank enables the bad behaviours of both characters. For example, Monica and Frank bring a group of people back home from a bar late at night, give beer to their underage son, and insist that the children party with them. On another occasion, Monica and Frank wake the children up in the middle of a school night to watch R-rated horror movies and eat candy while they pass a marijuana joint between them (season 2, episode 9 [Borstein 2012]).

As Monica works to gain the trust of her children, she discovers the "squirrel fund" Fiona has hidden in the cupboard and to which Fiona, Lip, Ian, Debbie, and Carl have all contributed to pay the household bills. Monica takes the money, and she and Frank spend it on drugs and a used Buick. Things take a turn for the worse as Monica's behaviour becomes more erratic, with her driving around with toddler Liam without a car seat and picking up Debbie from school while under the influence of drugs. Monica later allows Carl to drive, though he is underage, and he crashes the car and suffers a headwound, after which Monica is arrested.

At this point, Monica begins to descend into a manic state. After returning home from jail, Fiona confronts Monica for endangering Carl and once again expresses her disappointment (season 2, episode 10 [Frankel 2012]). In the following episode, Monica's depression worsens, and Frank tries to lift her spirits by giving her more drugs. Predictably, she gets worse, and during Thanksgiving dinner with everyone eating in the dining room, she attempts suicide in the kitchen. Not only does this act ruin the dinner everyone has laboured to prepare after Monica and Frank spent the household savings, Fiona worries that it has traumatized Debbie and Carl (season 2, episode 11 [Morgan and Pimental 2012]). Monica is placed in a psychiatric facility but once again leaves the family, running away with a fellow patient (season 2, episode 12 [Wells 2012]).

Following Monica's departure, her family goes through long periods of not knowing where she is. For example, in season 3, when social services remove the younger children from the family home, Fiona cannot find Monica and instead forges documents with her signature (season 3, episode 6 [Abbott and Wells 2013b]). Monica reunites with the family in season 7 (season 7, episode 9 [Wells 2016a]), but, after she and Frank renew their wedding vows and the family has a party, she dies (season 7, episode 10 [Wells 2016b]). Her death is attributed to a drug-related brain aneurism and therefore, it is indicated, a result of her own poor life choices (season 7, episodes 9–11 [Wells 2016a–c]). Fiona curses Monica's lifeless body while it lays in the coffin, indicting her profound resentment of her mother and the hardship she has caused. While Monica's behaviours are extreme in the few episodes when she does appear, the fact that she is a bad mother is reinforced explicitly in comments from other characters and evidenced by her absence throughout each season prior to her death.

It's Better When You're Gone

In both *Modern Family* and *Shameless*, the absent mothers are minor characters who left their families before the start of each show, enabling the premises of both shows. Both DeDe and Monica engage in a series of extreme personal choices that make their estrangements appear to be their own fault. The shows perform televisual alienation of the mother figure from the audience by disappearing her so that most of our knowledge of her is through the disparaging accounts of the main characters, and her behaviour during her actual appearances is beyond the pale. Other characters are allowed the opportunity to illustrate they are "good mothers," as they are seen doing the work of mothering while their own mothers are gone.

In both shows, the fathers of the family play a more prominent role than their ex-wives, even though they are flawed parents themselves. For example, though, like Monica, Frank often also disappears from his family, *Shameless* follows Frank when he is away: when he wakes up in Canada (pilot [Abbott and Wells 2011]) and Mexico (season 3, episode 1 [Abbott and Wells 2013a]), moves in with the character Shelia (season 1, episode 2 [Abbott 2011]), and spends many episodes drinking at his local bar, the Alibi Club. As the family notes, "he always comes back," whereas Monica's life is generally a mystery when she disappears (season 3, episode 1 [Abbott and Wells 2013a]), as is also the case for DeDe.

The characters' disappearing from the screen is one way in which audiences are alienated from Monica and DeDe, as the viewer's first-hand knowledge is limited to extreme episodes, and they must rely on accounts from other characters in their absence. This failure to follow mothers when they are away from their families is one technique of televisual alienation. As a point of contrast, the 2022 film *Lost Daughter*, based on the novel by Elena Ferrante, is told exclusively through the perspective of the mother figure, even when she leaves her family.

In life and death, DeDe and Monica are devices used to draw a contrast with the main characters who are present and seen selflessly caring for their family members. They are also vehicles used to create drama for the main characters and to facilitate personal growth for them. For example, Claire learns to appreciate her mother in all her complexity after she dies, illustrating that Claire has come to terms with her loss (season 11, episode 8 [Lloyd, Levitan, and Walls 2020). Though maternal deaths in *Modern Family* and *Shameless* facilitate grief for the main characters, the deaths of estranged mothers as ancillary but instrumental characters are not particularly tragic, indicating that the family is better off without them.

Maternal estrangements and absences can result from a variety of factors, not just the poor choices that (white) mothers make (Greenslade 2017). Given the prevalence of family estrangement and the trauma and stigma with which it is associated, more sensitive and complex popular cultural models are essential. New models can illustrate how to live and cope with the challenges and sense of loss that often accompany a mother's absence.

chapter six

Raised by a Menopausal Android: Middle-Age Rage and Maternal Futurism in *Raised by Wolves*

In season 1 of the HBO Max series *Raised by Wolves*, the central character known as Mother can make people explode with her piercing scream. She transforms into an indestructible, art-deco-like flying goddess and uses her super-human android strength to toss large men into the air. What middle-aged mother hasn't, at one time or another, wished for such powers? Once designed to be a killing machine called a Necromancer, Mother has been reprogrammed to focus on the reproductive labour of colonizing an apparently unpopulated planet, Keppler-22b, after Earth has been torn asunder by warring secular and religious factions. Mother's mission is to raise a cohort of six secular human children, the Generation 1s; but her children die one by one until only her son Campion remains alive. Following these deaths, Mother goes to great lengths to carry out her caregiving program and to populate her colony, abducting children aboard a spacecraft filled with a religious sect called the Mithraic (season 1, episode 2 [R. Scott 2020b]). This leads to further violence with the Mithraic, who attempt to reclaim their children. In the process of building a new society based on the models of Western civilization, Mother leaves death and destruction in her path. Despite her put-on smile and calm demeanor with the children, Mother faces mounting pressures and a myriad of insecurities in balancing her various roles.

As *Raised by Wolves* moralizes its dystopic conditions, it employs the cliché of the monstrous and increasingly unhinged woman transitioning out of her reproductive prime (Ussher 2006; Creed

1993). It also nods to Greco-Roman and Christian mythology around creation and destruction but, in doing so, it misses broader problematics related to the Western ontologies underpinning such stories, which have facilitated colonization, capitalism, and the exploitation of Earth and mothers alike (Deloria [1973] 2003). Further, the colonial narrative in the show is strange when considered in context. Racial dynamics are never addressed among the racially diverse cast of characters, including Mother, who is white-coded and leading the charge of colonizing this planet, and Father, her Black-male-coded counterpart, whom she dominates physically and intellectually.[1] The lack of critique around race is especially ironic considering the show was filmed in post-apartheid South Africa. While the show reaps the aesthetic benefits of a diverse cast, it erases the violence of this Black geography (McKittrick 2006) in its failure to address the implications of racial corporeality, marking it as a kind of post-race fantasy centred on Mother (C. Cohen 2011; Alexander-Floyd 2021; Kennedy 2017).[2] Despite her superpowers, it seems that Mother is still struggling with the age-old problems of Western society as well as those carried over from the second wave.

Raised by Wolves as Intertextual, Ontological, and Epistemological

If elements of *Raised by Wolves* sound familiar, it is because it is a highly intertextual show. Created by Aaron Guzikowski, the first two episodes were directed by the sci-fi giant Ridley Scott, who was also the executive producer on the show, helping to establish the tone and artistic direction (Essman 2020; Garcia and O'Falt 2021). As with some previous characters imagined by Scott, Mother is a strong, white, woman-coded heroine whose traversal between humanity, technology, and animality allows the show to engage with philosophical probes. Scott has previously played with similar forms and themes, which were clearly influenced by second wave feminism as well as Cold War undertones: the ingenious Ellen Ripley in *Alien* (1979), who fights an other-worldly monster and an android who turns on her, is one such example.[3] In *Bladerunner* (1982), Scott depicts super-human abilities via the acrobatic android Pris (played by Daryl Hannah) and questions the distinction between humanity and artificial intelligence through the femme fatale android Rachel (played by Sean Young). In *Prometheus*, the 2012 prequel to *Alien*, which references the Greek myth of the introduction of fire to humans, Scott depicts a story in which alien biology and technology form humanity, but the "engineers" who created humans in their image are far from benevolent gods.

In *Raised by Wolves*, similar themes intersect with motherhood and the messy business of creation stories. *Raised by Wolves*, like *Bladerunner*, raises age-old questions related to the human hubris of attempting to control nature and life, themes explored in the early nineteenth century in *Frankenstein; or, the Modern Prometheus* (Shelley [1818] 1999). By blurring the lines between technology and humanity and asking whether androids can love, have desire, or ever be trusted not to turn on humans, *Raised by Wolves* questions the nature of our relationship to the technologies (and offspring) we create and our ability and responsibility to control them once they are in the world. Moreover, by comparing humans to androids, it asks whether we can resist the blueprint of our very nature (or programming) and avoid our catastrophic destiny.

To explore these themes, the show employs not-so-subtle references to ancient Greek and Roman mythology and Christianity. For example, the story of Romulus and Remus is referenced throughout the show, from its title to the relic of Romulus's tooth carried by the Mithraic (season 1, episode 9 [Hawes 2020]). That ancient story tells of twin brothers who were said to have been fathered by Mars, the god of war, and who are classically depicted as suckling from a she-wolf. In keeping with the family tradition of violence, Romulus kills his brother and later founds Rome, illustrating man's propensity for conflict and competition. In the first season of *Raised by Wolves*, a similar story unfolds between Campion, who was raised to be secular, and another child, Paul, who may be a Mithraic prophet, which means that history could repeat itself on Kepler-22b (season 1, episode 3 [L. Scott 2020a]; season 1, episode 6 [Mimica-Gezzan 2020b]).

At the same time it depicts humans as inherently violent, *Raised by Wolves* reproduces long-standing tropes of the monstrous feminine through Mother in several ways including her more destructive powers. As with Medusa, who could turn men to stone with her gaze, looking upon Mother when she is weaponized can have dire results. And, like the sirens, who used their cries to lead sailors to their deaths (Ussher 2006; Creed 1993), Mother's screams can destroy men on the spot. Though going by the name Mother throughout the show, the character refers to herself as Lamia in one scene (season 1, episode 2 [R. Scott 2020b]); that is also the name of a child-eating monster who assumed many forms in Greek and European mythology, including a hybrid between animal and woman, and in some variations, half-woman, half-serpent or a quadruped (Zochios 2011; Sedinova 2016). In Greek mythology, Lamia conceived several children with Zeus, and all but one were killed by Zeus's angry wife, Hera. It was Lamia's grief that transformed her into a monster (Sedinova 2016). In *Raised by Wolves*, Mother's loss of her children is also transformational, and leads her to reassume her previous form as a weapon of mass destruction, illustrating motherhood driven to the brink by rage and grief (season 1, episode 1 [R. Scott 2020a]). Mother is also discovering that her body can do new and strange things that defy her understanding of her programming. As she learns, her creators did not fully understand the capacities of the mysterious "dark protons" with which they built her and which threaten to destroy everything (season 1, episode 8 [Gabassi 2000]).

In addition to depicting motherhood as out of control and dangerous, *Raised by Wolves* casts ambiguity around agency, matter, and technology, throwing into question the Cartesian assumption of cogito, which attributes agency only to humans (Coole and Frost 2010; Bennett 2010). Human war and hubris have meant the destruction of planet Earth, and, as humans bring their violence to the new planet as they colonize it, *Raised by Wolves* questions their ability to contain their own self-destruction and the alien environment in which they now find themselves. While the ever-logical atheists believe that individuals determine their own destiny with the help of science, the planet itself may have its own "immanent vitality" (Coole and Frost 2010, 8). New and unexplained occurrences veer into the supernatural and uncanny, such as when one of Campion's deceased sisters begins appearing as an apparition (season 1, episode 4 [L. Scott 2020b]; season 1, episodes 5 and 6 [Mimica-Gezzan 2020a and b]). New creatures also begin to stalk the children, and it is all Mother and Father can do to prevent the predators from eating them. Despite Mother's logical disposition as an android and a secularist, these strange happenings cannot be explained by science, and she cannot seem to control the natural environment around her.

We might read this difficulty as akin to the fear and anxiety reflected in many settler-colonial sites (Tuck and Yang 2012; Couthard 2014; Fischer-Tiné 2016). A colonial teleology is also echoed when Mother and Father discover that the planet may not be uninhabited after all. However, it seems their neighbours are pasty Neanderthals, making Mother's colonial telos seem less problematic than historical colonization on Earth because the new planet's inhabitants seem less human (season 1, episode 10 [L. Scott 2020c]).

Another particularly troubling storyline is that of Tempest, a Mithraic Black youth who becomes pregnant after being raped by a white-coded cleric. The cleric claims Sol (or God) directed him to commit this violence to propagate his seed (season 1, episode 8 [Mimica-Gezzan 2020a]). Tempest is deeply traumatized and resents her pregnancy, trying to kill herself. At the same time, she rejects many of the teachings of the Mithraic, who put the cleric in a position of power. Instead, she gravitates toward Mother, despite the fact that Mother abducted Tempest, murdering almost everyone aboard her ship (season 1, episode 8 [Gabassi 2020]; season 1, episode 9 [Hawes 2020]; season 1, episode 10 [L. Scott 2020c]). The implication that Tempest needs Mother to protect her (despite the violence Mother has perpetrated against her people) and to liberate her from an oppressive religion reproduces a sense of the white saviour complex, for which mainstream second wave feminism and Western civilization alike have been widely critiqued (Zakaria 2021).

The name "Tempest" may be a reference to Shakespeare's play *The Tempest*; even if that is not the case, there are still several parallels between the two works related to colonization and racial and gender dynamics. In the play, Prospero, a character who has been shipwrecked on an island with his daughter, Miranda, assumes mastery over the island's inhabitant, Caliban; in the process, he also assumes the role of "landholder," as he takes possession of the territory (Wynter 2006, 128). Black feminist literary scholar Sylvia Wynter (2000) critiqued the play as a narrative of Black enslavement and dispossession. She contends that, while Miranda is subjugated within a hierarchy of characters due to her gender, she assumes a higher ranking than Caliban, given her position as a white woman who is closer to the archetypal reasoning white subject/master, Prospero. Therefore, with respect to Caliban, she assumes a "legitimated expropriation of the right to endow his purpose" (2000, 114). Moreover, by evoking the possibility that Caliban will rape Miranda, the play feeds into long-standing white anxiety around white woman victimhood at the hands of Black men, reproducing the sexualization of Black men and their conflation with nature in the white psyche, which was used to justify slavery (Fanon [1952] 2008; Goldberg 2004).

Miranda is the only woman in the play, leading some Black feminist scholars to engage with key disappearances or, rather, the "absent presence" of Caliban's Black female counterpart, who never actually appears (Kynard 2012; McKittrick 2006).[4] Caliban's Black "woman" is so far outside the bounds of acceptable reason for Prospero that her materialization is foreclosed, and she is never made fully human in this white narrative (Wynter 2000). McKittrick (discussing Wynter's work) queries, "what would happen to our understanding and conception of race and humanness if black women legitimately inhabited our world and made their needs known?" (2006, xxv). Similarly, we might ask how the character Tempest would be constituted more fully if she were centred in *Raised by Wolves*.

In addition to attempts at smoothing out problematics around race and colonization by failing to acknowlege them, *Raised by Wolves* weaves a troubling epistemological framework in gesturing towards Biblical origin narratives in Genesis; in particular, the series offers a depiction of mankind as fundamentally flawed and at odds with his surroundings, which, as Standing Rock Sioux philosopher Vine Deloria Jr. ([1973] 2003) argued, underpins Western, Christian ontology. One episode hints at this narrative with the title "Lost Paradise" (season 1, episode 6 [Mimica-Gezzan, 2020b), a play on *Paradise Lost*, the 1667 poem by John Milton recounting the story of Adam and Eve in Genesis. In the Biblical story, God created Adam, and later created Eve from one of Adam's ribs. Eve then facilitated their downfall by succumbing to temptation by a serpent and convincing Adam to eat from the forbidden fruit. That act led to their expulsion from the Garden of Eden, staining all humankind in the eyes of God and dooming them to mortality on Earth. In this understanding, humankind is inherently flawed and is destined to atone for the original sin until the Second Coming of Jesus, which will mark the end of the world (Deloria [1973] 2003).

Deloria Jr. compares this Western understanding of humankind as fundamentally flawed and implicated in sin to many Indigenous belief systems where "man and the rest of creation are cooperative and respectful of the task set for them by the Great Spirit" with humans being "dependent on everything in creation" ([1973] 2003, 81). He makes another important distinction between Western and Indigenous ontologies: whereas Genesis charged humans with being the masters of animals and subduing the Earth, many Indigenous ontologies contextualize humans as one of many connected in a set of relations along with land, animals, plants, water, rocks, spirits of ancestors, and others around them on Earth, where they will continue to reside when they die (Deloria [1973] 2003). The latter perspective is reflected in the role of animals in many Indigenous stories and traditional knowledge specific to particular places, which still have salience in guiding Indigenous lifeways (Simpson 2011; Belcourt 2014). Deloria and others link the hierarchical Western belief system with environmental catastrophe. In addition to enabling environmental degradation, the Biblical treatment of man in Genesis as the steward of the land, women, and animals enabled the idea of private property, primitive accumulation, and gender-based exploitation for Western Christians (Federici 2004) as well as doctrines such as Terra Nullius and Manifest Destiny that were used to justify brutal colonization (Deloria [1973] 2003).[5]

Ironically, *Raised by Wolves* critiques the human propensity for self-destruction by employing the very mythologies that portray this as inevitable, including the *Bible* and Greco-Roman mythology. This employment misses the finer point that it is the ontological framework in which Western morality tales are implicated that has put humanity at odds with its surroundings in the first place. In the process, the dependence on problematic narratives reproduces creation myths that disappear Black women and degrade white women as the cause of man's original downfall, and mankind as her fundamentally damaged progeny. Mother's continual punishment and struggle are in keeping with this context, which is perhaps one of the reasons she is so angry.

"Keep Your Eyes Closed, Children. I'm Weaponized": White Mothering and Middle-Age Rage[6]

Despite its shortcomings, *Raised by Wolves* in many ways exhibits the progressive feminist fantasies imagined in Scott's previous work and by second wave feminists. Mother is the main character, and there is a division of reproductive labour and child rearing between Father and Mother. Father sometimes assumes the role of a nurturer, staying with the children while Mother ventures out to patrol (season 1, episode 8 [Mimica-Gezzana 2000a]). However, one of the sources of tension that Mother and Father face is that, while Father seems to provide more care than Mother to the children, Mother carries a heavier burden than Father in constituting and protecting the family, as Father is just a "generic service model" with less capacity (season 1, episode 3 [L. Scott 2020a]), despite having her well-being and that of the children as a central part of his programing (season 1, episodes 1 and 2 [R. Scott 2020a and b]). Several times throughout the show, Father indicates that he needs to feel more useful (season 1, episode 8 [Gabassi 2020]; season 1, episode 4 [L. Scott 2020b]). After Father sends a signal to the enemy Mithraic arc called "Heaven" when he is concerned that Campion will have no one to care for him when he and Mother stop functioning, Mother violently disables Father by impaling him, using her bare hand to reach into his chest and rip out his processer, which looks similar to a human heart. Mother is superior to Father in strength and sophistication and can easily dominate him physically (season 1, episode 1 [R. Scott 2020a]). This violent episode is just the beginning of some of Mother's more extreme behaviours in her role as a caregiver.

When the Mithraic arrive and attempt to take Campion from her, Mother converts back into a Necromancer and explodes them into oblivion. In what appears to be a drastically disproportionate response, she then ascends to the Mithraic arc and brutally murders several crewmembers while kidnapping five children in order to repopulate her colony and replace her dead children back on Kepler-22b. Finally, she sets the arc on a collision course, killing most of the remaining Mithraic onboard (season 1, episode 1 [R. Scott 2020a]).

After reactivating Father, Mother assures him that she was not acting rashly in killing the crew of the arc. She states that, contrary to his impression, "I never lost control. I just drew on a part of myself I didn't know existed" (season 1, episode 2 [R. Scott 2020b]). Mother further tries to gaslight Father by noting that "my actions served our core programming objective [to colonize Kepler-22b]" and that it was actually Father's attempt to call on the Mithraic to help care for Campion that had been a deviation from that objective (season 1, episode 2 [R. Scott 2020b]). He repeats back to her, as though trying to convince himself, "There was no loss of control" (season 1, episode 2 [R. Scott 2020b]). Mother repeats this same assurance about her absolute self-control to one of the Mithraic youth: "I have complete control over my mind's functioning, no matter what state I'm in" (season 1, episode 8 [Mimica-Gezzan 2020b]). However, Campion, who is increasingly influenced by the new Mithraic children, is less convinced and is disturbed by the scale of Mother's destruction and fits of rage and violence (season 1, episode 8 [Mimica-Gezzan 2020b]). As Mother is conflated with the archaic mother, the primordial beginning and ending of life (Kristeva 1982) and Lamia's vicious animality, she also becomes a monstrous mother, which, as Creed (1993) and others explain, reflects a patriarchal fascination, fear, and repulsion with respect to woman's reproductive capacities. Despite her confidence, Mother also soon begins to express doubts about her self-control (season 1, episode 3 [L. Scott 2020a]; season 1, episode 8 [Gabassi 2020]).

"Don't Worry Father. We'll Get It Right This Time": Faltering Fertility on a Barren Planet[7]

Adding to Mother's rage is her sense of grief at the loss of five of the six Generation 1 children. This grief is demonstrated through the expression of both animal and human-like emotions. When one of the children, Tally, is lured away from the settlement – to her death, it is presumed – Mother howls like a wolf in anguish (season 1, episode 1 [R. Scott 2020a]). She is equally devastated when she finds that the children have accidentally defrosted a batch of embryos, the Generation 2s, and they are no longer viable (season 1, episode 4 [L. Scott 2020b]). That Mother is failing in her core objective of realizing motherhood prompts her to go to horrific extremes to reach her goal of forming a family/colony of children. This quest finds parallels in many of the extreme measures some women use in their efforts to conceive, including invasive and expensive fertility treatments, insemination, in-vitro fertilization, and surrogacy (S. Lewis 2019). Like conventional conception, and potentially more so, these methods are difficult on bodies and emotionally taxing.

Technologically aided modes of conception are mimicked in *Raised by Wolves* shortly after Mother and Father land on Kepplar-22b, set up shelter, and begin the gestation process. Mother, whose naked body resembles a tan Barbie doll, with no discernible nipples or genitals, reclines on a bed. Father then initiates the umbilical process by using plastic tubes to connect Mother to six embryos situated in separate gelatin baths. The placement of the tube connectors is not unlike that of the nipples of a dog (or wolf), as they span two parallel rows of three along Mother's torso. Fluids flow from Mother to the embryos, until it is time to birth them. Father removes the newborns from the gelatin one by one, wrapping them and setting them down gently (season 1, episode 1 [R. Scott 2020a]).[8]

When it comes time for the last embryo to end its gestation, it is stillborn. Father notes that their programming tells them to break it down and feed it to the others; however, Mother objects and wants to hold the apparently dead fetus. She tenderly rocks it close to her rubber breast, and her singing and tears bring the infant back to life, after which they name him Campion. He will be the only child of the original six who survives (season 1, episode 1 [R. Scott 2020a]). The instincts and grief exhibited by mother, resembling that of a compassionate human mother, call into question whether Mother has relied on her programming and is emulating human behaviour, as we all do at times, or if she herself has become more human. Such a question has "implications for our understanding of the human as a distinctive biological or moral entity" (Coole and Frost 2010, 17).

While *Raised by Wolves* includes futuristic and creative forms of reproduction using androids, Mother's gestation period with the human embryos does not seem that far removed from surrogacy in its level of biomedical intervention, which circumvents the limitations of more conventional biological processes. Mother's struggle to reproduce after humans have destroyed the planet also parallels a drop in fertility associated with environmental contamination on Earth: Pizzorno (2018) notes that fertility is decreasing in industrialized countries due to metals and other pollutants in the environment that affect sperm count and ovulation as well as implantation and fetal viability.

The show's desolate, arid landscape and its references to the human-made destruction on Earth signal catastrophic climate change that is incompatible with human and animal life. From the opening credits of *Raised by Wolves*, we see satellite dishes vaporize with a nuclear blast, a bridge collapse, and a huge explosion in the atmosphere, all illustrating the extent of the damage caused by human-made technologies on Earth. Mother's previous role as a war machine implicates her in this desolation, a point made explicitly by a necromancer shown flying above the war-torn landscape in the opening sequence (Small 2020).

As Coole and Frost state, "questions regarding the definition, the ethical value, and the moral and political culpability of the human, the nonhuman, and the virtually human become especially vexed as concerns about environmental degradation and dwindling natural resources acquire an urgency unimaginable just a generation ago" (2010, 16).

In *Raised by Wolves*, with Earth a now uninhabitable planet, Mother is attempting to reproduce the human race within the dry, barren conditions of Kepler-22b. However, the infertile conditions of both the planet and her body signal a form of cultural abjection (Harrington 2018). Even though Mother is an android, she indicates a strong desire to be relegated into an acceptable gendered ideological order.

"Tell Me What You Want": Midlife Sexuality and Reproduction Out of Control[9]

In addition to her difficulties with infertility, new and unexpected changes experienced by Mother can be read as a sign of menopausal transition onset, "a gradual transition through decreasing fertility to complete termination of menses" (Moseley, Druce, and Turner-Cobb 2020, 1432). The National Institute for Health and Care Excellence (2015) lists, among other symptoms of the menopausal transition, effects on mood (due to hormonal fluctuations and decrease in estrogen), sexual difficulties, and urogenital symptoms like vaginal dryness (for which the desert climate of Keppler-22b is an apt metaphor). Although Amanda Collin, the actress who plays Mother, was only thirty-four when the series premiered in 2020 (IMDb 2022), this is, by Hollywood standards, middle aged for a woman, and the age of perimenopause onset for some. The short, no-hassle haircut (which resembles that of Rosemary Woodhouse after she becomes pregnant and begins to mature) also seals Mother's midlife positioning.

Mother is indeed noticing new and surprising changes to her body, an experience to which many women transitioning through menopause can relate. In addition, Mother's mood is changing, and she is increasingly irritated with Father and Campion (season 1, episode 3 [L. Scott 2020a]; season 1, episodes 5 and 6 [Mimica-Gezzan 2020a and b]). While Father eagerly awaits her returns when she is on patrol and wants nothing more than to please her, as per his programming, Mother is despondent and less patient with him (season 1, episode 5 [Mimica-Gezzan 2020b]). She is also increasingly perturbed at Campion's newfound rebellion against her as he begins to doubt her actions and secular teachings due to the influences of his new Mithriac friends (season 1, episode 3 [L. Scott 2020a]). Moreover, while apparently programmed to act strictly in accordance with her mission, Mother seems to be facing a new and unexpected sexual awakening. Though she remarks to Tempest, "I'm not one that wants. I'm one who serves" (season 1, episode 6 [Mimica-Gezzan 2020b]), Mother soon begins to exhibit her own desires, as marked by increasingly erratic and careless behaviours that seem more human than android, reflecting signs of a midlife crisis.

Rather than spending time patrolling as she says she is when Father asks, Mother secretly begins frequenting a simulator where she (re)enacts a virtual romantic relationship with the man who apparently programmed her, Campion Sturges (season 1, episode 5 [Mimica-Gezzan 2020a]). Her feelings for Sturges grow, and they have a virtual sexual affair; she is, in essence, being unfaithful to Father, who is already feeling inadequate because he is unable to protect their children. Not only is Mother failing as a nurturer, but she also falters in her parental partnership, further adding to her confusion and crisis of purpose. Because she lets her guard down while in the simulator, Mother leaves herself, Father, and the children vulnerable to an attack from the Mithraic in the episode titled "Lost Paradise" (season 1, episode 6 [Mimica-Gezzan 2020b]).

As Jane Ussher notes, sexuality in aging women has long been a trope in horror. "If the older woman is depicted as alive, as sexual, this in itself makes her an object of fascination (or disgust), threatening again to evoke the fear of the feminine, of the devouring, powerful Medusa who is sexual outside the control of men" (2006, 119). Mother's body is not treated as abject in her sexual encounter, but it is when, following that encounter, she discovers that she is pregnant, an outcome intentionally planned by unknown actors. Perhaps like many mothers at this life stage facing an unplanned pregnancy, Mother is shocked and dismayed, especially as it was conceived without her consent, not unlike the pregnancy in *Rosemary's Baby* (season 1, episode 8 [Gabassi 2020]).[10] And, as with Rosemary Woodhouse – an unwitting subversion of the Virgin Mary – Mother is confused and guilty in the aftermath of what has happened to her, saying "I allowed myself to be invaded. Neglected my mission, my family" (season 1, episode 8 [Gabassi 2020]). Like Rosemary's new and surprising penchant for raw meat while pregnant, Mother begins to surprise herself with an animal-like craving for blood to feed the alien fetus growing inside her. In addition to sniffing around (like a wolf) for blood, she licks her hand after killing one of the planet's indigenous creatures, then using it to transfuse blood into her own body. This impulse seems illogical and surprising to her, as her body generally is nourished with a white fuel (season 1, episode 8 [Gabassi 2020]).

Mother's inability to control her own reproduction and her discovery of new things that her body can do (such as carry a pregnancy) indicates a vitality of her body and a blurring of human traits, fabricated material, and artificial intelligence (Coole and Frost 2010; Bennett 2010). Like Tempest, she is disturbed by her lack of consent in the process as well as with the child that emerges. Like Athena, who violently hammered her way out of the skull of her father, Zeus, Mother's offspring emerges in a shocking way, moving from a lump in her abdomen, up through her throat, and exiting through her mouth as a giant, flying serpent with concentric rows of teeth like a sea lamprey, which it uses to attach itself to her side to feed (season 1, episode 10 [L. Scott 2000c]). Her progeny and her body have assumed their own agency, using her as a mere vessel. (Many mothers likely feel this way through pregnancy and breastfeeding, as their bodies transform and their offspring express their own formidable will.)

Like Rosemary, Mother is horrified by the creature she has produced and worries that it might begin to feed on humans after it is done with her. In keeping with the biblical analogy, female sexual curiosity and desire (as symbolized in Genesis by the eating of forbidden fruit) have dire consequences, and not just for the woman herself. Mother and Father atone for her mistake by setting themselves on a suicide collision course, along with Mother's serpent-like offspring, in the hope of saving what humans are left. As the season comes to a close, Mother and Father have sacrificed themselves for humanity and can only hope that the humans manage not to destroy themselves again (season 1, episode 10 [L. Scott 2000c]).

"You Are the New Mother of Humanity. Save Us": *Catapulting towards Catastrophe*[11]

Season 1 of *Raised by Wolves* leaves us with many questions. First, if humans continue to reproduce the same age-old conflicts and destruction that date back to the beginnings of Western civilization, what is the point of saving them? While humankind has attempted to offset its own destruction through new and more extreme means of reproduction, has it been worth it? Is mothering futile if humans insist on destroying their environments and themselves? Our responses to these questions – and the other questions we may ask – will likely vary depending on our ontological positioning.

   Despite her new superpowers, Mother is still punished, she still struggles, and she still inflicts violence on others. Her body and emotions are out of control, she is enraged, she is underappreciated by her family and society, she still feels like she has to do everything herself, she sometimes feels unhinged regardless of her self-assurance, she experiences disenfranchised grief, and she is disappointed in Father. Yet, at least she exists, both visually and discursively, as an active, albeit flawed, agent. While the promises of second wave feminism have allowed Mother to be the main provider for and protector of the family, as well as the main character, this has not led to liberation for anyone. But, this is not destiny; it is just another story told by man.

chapter seven

A Long Way from Liberation

It's time to finish my manuscript. I've been holed up in this hotel for eighteen hours. I'm hiding from my family and my colleagues under the guise of an out-of-town conference, which I have skipped for the day. I've been living on caffeine and a giant box of IKEA cookies, emerging from my room only for more coffee pods. I'm ignoring my emails and texts. These are the conditions I have orchestrated in order to concentrate. Housekeeping employees politely call me "ma'am" when I walk down the hallways. The irony is not lost on me that my labour involves sitting in the same place tapping away neurotically at my keyboard while they do manual labour – me, a white person from the United States, and them, racialized, precarious labourers from the Philippines. I feel guilty about the inequity, but know I need to complete the task at hand. I am writing about reproductive labour and motherhood, but that feels far away now.

At home, my mother-in-law has made a special trip to help care for my children while I'm gone. If I were there, I would be distracted by any number of daily responsibilities: getting kids out the door to school; coordinating with van drivers, respite workers, teachers, my spouse, the handyman; feeding people; bathing people; doing laundry; doing more laundry; toilet training; dressing kids; making dinner; packing lunches; unpacking lunches; washing dishes; grocery shopping; taking care of sick family members; and engaging in bedtime rituals. On most mornings, I open my computer to start my paid labour following two to three hours of unpaid work. But here, it is quiet. I am focused.

I began this book shortly before the pandemic. It took shape first as discrete ideas whose interconnections gradually congealed across time. It was hammered out in moments of desperation during COVID lockdowns. Shift work with my kids would start with me around 6 a.m., my partner would take over in the afternoon, when I would get the bulk of my paid work done, then me again in the evening. We lived together, but I barely saw him. We both had paid labour to balance with domestic labour. I would fall into bed sometime around 11 p.m. just to do it all again the next day. "I don't know if I'm going to make it," I would say to myself sometimes. Even when performed in stolen, tactical moments, the writing was my solace. It was like exiting my body temporarily to look back from a detached distance. Exhaustion; no end in sight; write, write, write. Paid and unpaid work blurred together into one endless day. I loved my kids. I was lucky to have a job in a time of global crisis. But I did not feel lucky.

Learning about Wages for Housework was a revelation. Years before my struggles, this and other second wave movements had denaturalized modern conditions of production and reproduction and the crushing banality that often constitutes them. I came to understand that my experiences were not unique. While exponentially worse during COVID-19, my conditions were neither isolated to the pandemic nor particular to my social circumstances. And, in fact, for many people, circumstances were much, much worse.

Feminists had been demanding meaningful change for decades. But, as discussed throughout the book, mainstream second wave goals to achieve gender equity in waged work overshadowed other feminist possibilities. The competition among strategies (Toupin 2018), in combination with a conservative backlash in the 1980s, worked to obscure many of the meaningful aims of second wave movements, including those that more fully addressed interlocking systems of oppression (Combahee River Collective [1977] 2017). In the process, Wages for Housework and other strategies that acknowledged reproductive labour *as* labour were sidelined and never gained prominence. While access to paid employment is important, the missed opportunity to validate the work performed by mothers, and mothers themselves, is part and parcel of an economic system that valorizes the ideal wage earner. This system ignores the social worlds in which workers exist and the labour necessary to sustain them and human life. These erasures, combined with the persistence of mother blame as part of a devaluation of motherwork, continue to cause trouble for all mothers.

Critical readings of the themes raised during the second wave are as relevant as ever. Continuing to remember them will help us make interventions in contemporary feminist agendas and ensure that concerns of mothering are at the forefront of public discourse. As mainstream feminisms have shifted their focus to positionality and worked to "disrupt a white, heteronormative, middle-class view" (Rivers 2017, 10), Motherhood studies has also widened its focus, expanding beyond critiques of patriarchal motherhood (Rich 1976) to those of normative motherhood encompassing intersecting concerns (O'Reilly 2023). This is an important step in acknowledging that patriarchy is not the only systemic feature of oppression that affects contemporary mothers. But while many feminists understand the third and fourth waves as important forms of distancing from the second, which are often characterized by infighting between older and younger generations (Rivers 2017), this book implores us not to abandon the various forms of second wave activism ignited so long ago. The current post-feminist notion that feminism is either a fait accompli or irrelevant today (Rivers 2017) underlines the urgency of a historically grounded understanding of feminism and the place of mothers within it.

Equally challenging in ensuring that mothers are not excluded from feminist conversations will be continued critique of their more problematic inclusions in the popular imaginary. As chapter 3 on HGTV mothers indicated, more positive post-feminist discourses of motherhood, while a seeming departure from mother blame, are, in reality, equally damning. This brand of motherhood discourse is marked by the emergence of "marketplace feminism," a form of post-feminist empowerment that is highly commodified, individualistic, and oriented around financial success (Rivers 2017, 75). The post-feminist orientation emphasizes ideas of "choice and empowerment," but importantly, as Rivers discusses, having a choice is not, in and of itself, feminist, and neither are all the choices on offer (ibid.). Moreover, if the emergent fourth wave is largely characterized by its existence online (Munro 2013), we must more fully understand it within the longer legacies of platform activism, where minoritized voices and bodies have been marginalized (Singh and Sharma 2019).

Regardless of whether fourth wave feminism has arrived or is eminent (Rivers 2017), it is a crucial time to intervene and stress the place of mothers within feminist debates as those debates take shape. In doing so, and in order to continue to open up Motherhood studies along with feminisms, popular manifestations of motherhood must remain an important point of critique. As this book has argued, white motherhood as a sensibility is ubiquitous in popular media and discourse. This form of motherhood accepts neoliberal logic and validates an economic structure that clearly values and benefits some and not others. At the same time, it erases people of colour doing the work of mothering, whether of their own children or those of others.

As *Mother Trouble* has illustrated, white mothers in our popular imaginary seem vexed with anxieties, despite their racial privilege and hyper-visibility; this reflects anxieties around the unfulfilled hopes and omissions of the second wave as we inhabit our current feminist wave and intensified neoliberal conditions. Patriarchy, sexism, and male ineptitude are still often identified as the sources of mother trouble, when the trouble is not mothers themselves, of course. The solutions offered – just push back against a sexist boss or be your own #momboss – reinforce the long-standing trope of mother blame when maternal troubles persist. While most certainly an insidious problem underpinning the institution of motherhood, a singular focus on patriarchy ignores other systemic problems. The trouble of motherhood is not simply patriarchy, but the interlocking economic conditions that enable patriarchy and white supremacy to flourish, as some second wave activists argued.

Taking a long view, focusing on a discursive trajectory across a historical span and media forms, has helped to illustrate the ways in which motherhood as an institution has both transformed and remained consistent. We started with *Rosemary's Baby* from the late 1960s and ended with *Raised by Wolves* of 2020. Rosemary, like Joanna Eberhart of *The Stepford Wives*, was subordinated in relation to her husband, who worked outside of the home in waged labour. While Joanna was partially right that the men (or patriarchy) were behind her oppression, neither Joanna nor Rosemary seemed fully cognizant of their exploitation in the process of reproducing wage relations. Moreover, both women seemed oblivious to their own racial and class privilege. While Rosemary felt profoundly uncomfortable with people of colour – for example, the Black "laundresses" relegated to the shadows of her basement, and her elevator operator, who was seen but not heard – Joanna is mildly interested in forming an allyship against the patriarchy with the Black literary figure Ruth Hendry in Ira Levin's novel, but this more fully developed depiction of Hendry never makes it to the screen. If we push beyond the gender-based critiques in chapter 2 to discuss the racial hierarchy and wage relations in which Rosemary and Joanna were positioned vis-à-vis scantly referenced Black characters and labourers, we can see this as a metaphor for the omissions and competing claims of second wave feminism.

These problems persist fifty years later in *Raised by Wolves*, a futuristic series adorned with a somewhat progressive veneer. As discussed in chapter 6, the show can be read as a metaphor for the continuing omissions of the second wave. Mother in *Raised by Wolves* has made some headway in the gender hierarchy as the definitive head of her multiracial family. However, she falls victim to the old trope of the unhinged monstrous mother, and, like Rosemary, is reduced to a uterus and exploited for her reproductive capacities, a fate consistent with the nightmare of capitalism described by Mariarosa Dalla Costa ([1972] 2016).[1] Like Rosemary, Mother seems to miss the broader racial politics in her own relative relations of power as the show assumes a post-race aesthetic and is driven by a colonial narrative. And, while the cast is multiracial, *Raised by Wolves* continues the erasure of people of colour in *Rosemary's Baby* by centring Mother and flattening racial difference.

Chapter 4 encouraged us to consider the ways in which "bad" mothers (Karens and anti-vaxx moms) help to reinscribe acceptable modes of (white) motherhood. In doing so, it asks us to think about the knock-on effects of countering problematic discourses like neurotypicality, vaccine conspiracies, and white entitlement with more problematic tropes about bad mothers; this form of mother blame continues a long-standing double bind that attributes broad social problems to mothers and condemns them for their failures to solve them. It is probably no accident that fathers, or anti-vaxx Chads, are much less salient signifiers in the Reddit memes discussed in chapter 4, as it is much easier to blame Karen. It seems that part of the "unfinished business" of feminism is mother blame, which transcends both pro- and anti-vaxx sentiment (O'Reilly 2014, 51).

Similarly, in examining the complex phenomenon of family estrangement, chapter 5 asked readers to consider the ways in which popular television shows encourage us to reproduce mother blame by attributing estrangement to the bad choices made by white mothers who opt out of reproductive labour. But such a focus on the shortcomings of white mothers omit other key reasons for absent mothers of all races, including intergenerational trauma, racism, the incarcerations disproportionately experienced by women of colour and Indigenous women (Major 2021), socio-economic disparities, illness and death related to social determinants of health, and participation in the global flows of reproductive labour (Duffy 2007; Henaway 2023).

As chapter 3 discussed, home renovation and design reality television presents a similarly skewed version of motherhood, in this case reproducing the expectations of flexible labour through the discourse of entrepreneurial motherhood. In such shows, audiences of (mostly white) mothers are encouraged to interpellated the ideals of "good" neoliberal motherhood with the hallmarks of private property and flexible labour. But this perspective conceals the injustice of precarious labour and housing for those of a lower socio-economic status, and especially Black, Latinx, and Indigenous mothers, who are much less likely to purchase a home (CMHC 2021b) and, unlike these HGTV moms, may not be able to bring their children to work with them (Vandenbeld Giles 2020).

The intention of this book was not to prescribe gender ideals or to valorize motherhood as a preordained compulsory calling, but to turn a critical lens on those forms and discourses of mother-hood that are most frequently depicted in popular culture. I have explored mediations of largely white cisgender mothers, rather than Black or Indigenous mothers, trans or queer mothers, and motherwork more broadly. And, there is a plethora of other texts and issues focusing on white mothers with which this book could have engaged – for example, the films *Mother!*; *Lost Daughter*; and *Three Billboards Outside Ebbing, Missouri*; and television shows like *The Maid, Mom, 19 Kids and Counting*, and *Workin' Moms*. It also could have studied transmediated internet sensations like #IMOMSOHARD.[2]

Regardless of such limitations, the troubles explored in this book apply to many mothers. Many of us struggle with misogyny, aging, and the treatment of our aging bodies as abhorrent. Many of us struggle with a lack of support, ableism, and disenfranchised grief. Those who shoulder more of the reproductive labour under capitalism will always be undervalued and exploited when profit, rather than caring for people, is the bottom line.

As younger generations feel less pressure to take on conventional gender roles, perhaps this will change. Many adult Generation Zs and millennials face an uncertain future marked by economic pre-carity, climate change, and political unrest (Petersen 2019; Cairns 2017). Some have recognized the untenable conditions of contem-porary motherwork and have very reasonably decided to opt out, see opting in as an impossibility – or perhaps they simply do not resonate with the "cult of motherhood." This may especially be the case if they are aware of the exhausting and disproportionate level of reproductive labour in which mothers are currently entrenched. Regardless of the reasons, in Canada, which is considered a "low fertility" country, people are having fewer children, and, like the United States, they are having them at an older age compared with previous generations (Statistics Canada 2018; Morse 2022).

So why should the unrealized dreams of second wave femi-nism matter to younger generations? Second wave movements were far from homogeneous, and they offered many imaginative potential futures (Romney 2021; Combahee River Collective [1977] 2017; Boyer 1997); there is still a lot we can learn from them.[3] They

encouraged women to decide whether to have children, to participate in the labour force, or to do both. They imagined a better overall distribution of labour and social and community supports, like
free or affordable childcare (Davis 1981; James 2012), which would
also enable us to avoid the pitfalls of treating families and children
as private property (Barrett and McIntosh 1982; S. Lewis 2019) and
motherhood as a siloed institution that must be shouldered alone
(Rich 1976; Barrett and McIntosh 1982). They argued for accessible
and legal reproductive healthcare (Taylor 2017; Romney 2021).
They argued against imperialism, colonialism, homophobia, and
racism (Third World Women's Alliance [1971] 2016; Taylor 2017).
They argued against gender-based violence (Campbell, Dawson,
and Gidney 2022). Acknowledging the role of all of these issues
in social struggles related to feminism and motherhood can help
prevent the same mistakes and false starts ad infinitum.

So, the struggle continues. Mothers are still the unfinished business of feminism. However, there is a way to demand necessary
change while avoiding the universalization of motherhood and the
hierarchies of capitalism. If anything, we need fresh approaches
that open up practices of mothering and find meaningful support
expanding beyond, but not abandoning, gender equity. If we look
back at the unfulfilled hopes and omissions of the second wave
as well as movements that valued reproductive labour and prioritized mothering as it relates to whole communities, perhaps then
we can imagine a better future for the work that mothers do.

Notes

1. Unfinished Business

1 It is worth noting that many women of colour and of lower socio-economic standing performed both paid and unpaid domestic labour. Moreover, as discussed further in chapter 2, Wages for Housework did not just advocate compensation for invisible labour, but was also a strategy that sought to disrupt rather than reproduce capitalism by pointing out its naturalized exploitation (Toupin 2018; Dalla Costa [1972] 2016). As Toupin states, "in a word, to demand wages for housework constituted a lever of power to open negotiations on the *conditions of reproduction*" (53, emphasis in original).

2 In Canada in 2015, mothers of at least one child under eighteen earned $.85 for every dollar earned by men, while women without children earned $.90 (Moyser 2017).

3 As Toupin (2018) points out, the universal family allowance instituted in England following the advocacy of Eleanor Rathbone, was transferred to Canada in 1944; however, it was peeled back in favour of tax credits in the 1980s. Rathbone's model varied from a universal basic income (McKay 2001), as she insisted that the allowance go to the mothers rather than the wage earners in a household, who were generally men (Toupin 2018).

4 As Campbell, Dawson, and Gidney (2022) note, there is some debate around the metaphors and demarcation of feminist movements. While noting some of the difficulties of characterizing feminism temporally, they suggest the generally accepted period of first wave feminism as from the mid- to late nineteenth century to approximately 1920; second wave feminism from the mid-1960s to the early 1980s; and the third wave from the early 1990s, reflecting the term coined by Walker in 1992 to

reject the idea of post-feminism or the idea that gender equality had been achieved. They also note that some feminists argue that we are currently experiencing a fourth wave marked by online activism (citing Munro 2013). Though beyond the scope of this book, further considerations could be given to the nuances between Canadian and U.S.-based feminisms (Campbell, Dawson, and Gidney 2022).

5 The idea of the mother figure is used periodically throughout this book. Sobchack ([1996] 2015) points out that "figures" "visibly represent the origin and process of narrative" (175). They continue, "Figures coalesce, condense, embody, enact, and transform the trouble in the text, the narrative problematic," though they also serve to "alter it, to describe it differently from its previous visible articulations" (175). Following this definition, I consider the mother figure and variations on it (e.g., the matriarch or the Karen figure as anti-vaxx mom) to be visual and discursive forms imbued with meaning that are subject to change, depending on cultural, political, and historical context.

6 For example, the white "refrigerator mother" whose emotional withdrawal caused her children to be autistic, according to experts such as Leo Kanner and Bruno Bettelheim (Douglas and Klar 2020; Plant 2010).

7 By "post-feminist," I mean the "notion that women's equality has been fully achieved" following the second wave (Campbell, Dawson, and Gidney 2022, 9).

8 Other clear advantages include being cisgender, straight, healthy, able-bodied, neurotypical, and in a heteronormative, two-parent relationship with children who have low support needs.

9 Toupin summarizes this position as follows: "Paying women for their domestic and childcare work, it was maintained, would only perpetuate their status of dependence in the family …. The egalitarians preferred to demand equal wages, greater commitment by men to fatherhood, and sharing and socialization of domestic tasks" (2018, 45).

10 A version of chapter 2 was previously published as "'I Think the Men Are Behind It': Reproductive Labour and the Horror of Second Wave Feminism," *Feminist Media Studies* (2020), https://doi.org/10.1080/14680777.2021.19860 93. Reprinted courtesy of Taylor and Francis Ltd.: www.tandfonline.com/. A version of chapter 4 was also previously published: Miranda J. Brady, Erica Christiansen, and Emily Hiltz. "Good Karen, Bad Karen: Visual Culture and the Anti-vaxx Mom on Reddit," *Journal of Gender Studies* (2022). © 2022 The Authors. Published by Informa UK Limited, trading as Taylor and Francis Group, https://doi.org/10.1080/09589236.2022.2069088. The version in this book has been adapted from the original article.

11 It is important to note that I assume an affirmation/social model of disability and avoid a deficit model, wherein parents see their disabled children as a burden (Swain and French 2000). However, it is also important to point out the lack of support for caregivers and the relegation (and devaluation) of so-called unproductive bodies to the private sphere. Caregiving for elderly, ill, or disabled family members is treated as an individualized responsibility and overwhelmingly falls to women (Tong 2007).

2. "I Think the Men Are Behind It"

1 The chapter title is taken from a line of dialogue by protagonist Joanna Eberhart (Katharine Ross) in the 1975 film *The Stepford Wives* who is telling her psychologist, Dr. Francher (Carole Eve Rossen), that she believes the members of the Stepford Men's Association are plotting against their wives.

2 In 1977 Polanski was arrested and convicted for the statutory rape of a thirteen-year-old girl, only one of several sexual assaults for which he is now publicly known, though he has avoided prison and has enjoyed a successful career (Alderman and Peltier 2019).

3 In one scene from the book (but not in the film), Rosemary enters the basement to do laundry and finds a group of "negro laundresses" who had been talking but who suddenly go quiet as she enters. "She had smiled all around and tried to be invisible, but they hadn't spoken another word and she had felt self-conscious, clumsy, and Negro oppressing" (Levin [1967] 2017, 28–9). Additionally, in a series of hallucinations, she tries to warn a "Negro mate" steering a ship they share that they are headed towards a typhoon. However, her warnings go ignored, as she "saw at once that he hated all white people, hated her," even though he treated her in a "courteous" manner (Levin [1967] 2017, 95–6).

4 At the time, abortion was already legally practised in New York (Reagan 1997). *Griswold v. Connecticut* (1965) and *Baird. v. Eisenstadt* (1972) used the privacy argument to protect the right to use oral contraceptives. *Roe v. Wade* (1973) also acknowledged the constitutional right to privacy – in this case, as protecting a woman's right to have an abortion. In 2022, the US Supreme Court ruled that the constitutional right to privacy argument did not apply to abortion and overturned *Roe v. Wade*, a decision that was preceded and followed by protests demanding that women's right to abortion continue to be recognized (Stolberg 2020; Totenberg and McCammon 2022).

5 Although Rosemary later learns she was mistaken about the circumstances of her rape, it is important to note Guy's culpability, as he facilitated and participated in Rosemary's physical and psychological violation.

6 As Ryan (1995) notes, the state of California did not overturn the marital rape exemption until 1980. Though Brownmiller (1975) is cited here as an important text related to marriage and rape, it is important to note the book was critiqued for a failure to focus on the oppression of marginalized men; some argued that it painted Black men as rapists (Edwards [1976] 2016).

7 This braless trend was marked during the 1968 Miss America Pageant, when women's liberation protesters threw their bras in the trash as they demonstrated against women's objectification (Echols 2002). However, while women's liberation activists contested hyper-femininity and submissiveness, the actresses in the filmic version of *The Stepford Wives* (even those identifying as feminist) were made to conform to the male gaze as heteronormatively attractive women in revealing clothing through which their nipple are exposed (Foertsch 2019), and this also effectively reduces feminist perspectives to popular aesthetic choices.

8 In the film, Joanna's husband, Walter, makes this comment about Carole after eating a casserole she has prepared.

9 When Joanna visits her friend Charmane after her apparent conversion, she is wearing perfume that smells like Walter's mother's, indicating that the men of Stepford want a sexier version of their mothers.

3. Mother Hustle

1 In noting performances of motherhood, I am referencing both Judith Butler's (1990) description of gender as performative and Adrienne Rich's seminal book *Of Women Born* (1976), which describes socially inscribed expectations for mothers in patriarchal motherhood.

2 Despite the pervasiveness of multitasking for women, it went unmeasured in national survey data until 2010. In 2015, nearly 20 per cent of women in Canada performed housework and/or caregiving at the same time as leisure activities, as opposed to 6 per cent of men. Arguably, this would make their leisure time (which constitutes about thirty minutes less per day than men) (Moyser and Burlock 2018) more fragmented and less relaxing.

3 According to its website, the corporation, "focuses on encouraging strategic business partnerships among the converging cultural media

industries, including film and television production, book and magazine publishing, sound recording and interactive digital media. In addition to fostering partnerships, the agency seeks to address the distance challenges each of the cultural industries faces in domestic and international marketplaces" (https://www.pas.gov.on.ca/Home/Agency/406).

4 For example, in a *Making It Home* episode, Kortney Wilson shops online with a client for a dining room table on The Brick website, and then mentions the retailer again later in the episode (season 2, episode 2 [Zalameda 2021]).

5 In addition to financial support through Canadian funding, the couple tapped further into the Canadian celebrity apparatus, winning Canadian Screen Awards in 2016, 2017, and 2018.

6 Although Joanna Gaines identifies as half Asian (her mother is Korean) and half Caucasian (Weisholtz 2021), white consumers are an important audience for her: as this chapter discusses, homeowners constitute a huge audience for her brand (Meredith Corporation 2022), and white homeownership far surpasses that of racial minorities (CMHC 2021b). I would also argue that the soft modernist style (Rosenberg 2011) employed by Gaines (e.g., intentionally distressed barn doors and antiques), which is generic enough to appeal widely, erases signs of any particular ethnicity or race and reproduces a ubiquitous whiteness.

7 Newer shows like *Good Bones* and *Help I Wrecked My House* assume a slightly different format, where husbands or male partners of cisgender woman hosts Mina Starsiak and Jasmine Roth, respectively, are much less visible. However, the performance of motherhood is still a part of such shows, from the time of the hosts' pregnancy to the appearance of their small children onscreen.

4. Good Karen, Bad Karen

1 Please see chapter 1, note 5 for the definition of "figure" employed in this book.

2 Though several web forums circulate memes, Reddit is a prominent space in the attention economy and a convenient site for access to debates over modern vaccination, during the time leading up to COVID-19. At the time of writing, the content of Reddit's posts are not reviewed or censored, as on other social media websites.

3 Autism spectrum disorder, otherwise known simply as autism, is defined as a neurological "disorder" in the Diagnostic and Statistical Manual of Mental

Disorders (DSM-5) (American Psychiatric Association 2013). However, it is treated very differently among self-advocates who resist medicalized models and understand autism as a form of neurological difference and an important social identity with its own benefits (Yergeau 2018).

4 The Ken or Chad figures sometimes referenced in partnership with Karen further emphasize this heterosexual construction (Berical 2021). Our sample did not feature Ken or Chad figures.

5 These posts generated heightened levels of user activity – with 32.6 thousand and 21.9 thousand upvotes, some of the highest levels of user activity in the analytical sample.

5. Disappearing Mom

1 Take, for example, the first film in the *Home Alone* franchise, where the lonely character, "Old Man Marley," is reunited with his granddaughter in a heartwarming scene at the end, just in time for everyone to celebrate Christmas together. In a more recent example, the Disney film *Encanto* included a family member named Bruno who had disappeared/was ostracized because of the perception that his presence was harmful to the family (Howard and Bush 2021). However, they are reunited, and the family accepts Bruno after he helps avert a crisis. The song from the film "We Don't Talk about Bruno" (Miranda 2021) became a surprise hit on the Billboard Hot 100 in early 2022 and is also very popular on TikTok, potentially because it includes themes with which many families are familiar, including marginalization, alienation, and estrangement of some members who do not fit in (Weaver 2022).

2 *Modern Family* was ranked the number two television show in Canada in 2020 in a Top 10 chart produced by FlixPatrol reporting most-streamed shows by country on Netflix (Moore 2020), and *Shameless* season 11 was reported to be the fourth most-watched TV show streaming on Netflix in the United States from 11 to 17 October 2021 (Netflix 2021; Meek 2021). Netflix began publishing data on its top 10 streaming TV shows and films starting from 28 June 2021 (Netflix 2021).

3 "Absent presence" can be defined as "the discernible influence of a particular individual on some social or textual practice even when they are not present" (definition from Oxford Reference, www.oxfordreference .com/display/10.1093/oi/authority.20110803095344811;jsessionid=0250D 2BFACF5C4DDFCAD490539D17624.

4 Absent or deceased mothers are a recurring narrative trope and represent a transhistorical phenomenon. Of the potential reasons for maternal

disappearances, such story lines allow fathers the opportunity to form closer bonds with their children (perhaps a paternal fantasy), force children to grow up rapidly, and create conflicts in need of resolution (Astrom 2017).

5 In the show, Carl is problematically depicted as intellectually impaired, with a lack of empathy (Aspler, Harding, and Cascio 2022) – for example, he tortures animals (see the pilot episode [Abbott and Wells 2011]) and attempts to murder a cousin with rat poison (season 3, episode 7 [Abbott and Wells, 2013c]). As Linda Blum (2007) points out, mothers of children with disabilities, including those that are invisible, often share stigma with their children. FASD is a neurological difference that is particularly stigmatized and stereotyped, associated with both mother blame and lower socio-economic status (Aspler, Harding, and Cascio 2022).

6. Raised by a Menopausal Android

1 Mother is played by white Danish actress Amanda Collin, and Father is played by Abubakar Salim, a Black, British-born actor.

2 We might compare this aesthetic of Black inclusion to Canada's politics of recognition of Indigenous people as critiqued by Couthard (2014) and more recently Adese (2022). As they note, while such highly visible inclusions bolster the nation's sense of multiculturalism, they elide more meaningful political action like land repatriation.

3 The central computer for Ripley's spacecraft in *Alien* was also called "Mother." At one desperate point in the film, she calls it a "bitch." She also calls the alien a "son of a bitch" (R. Scott 1979).

4 See chapter 5, note 3 for a definition of "absent presence."

5 In Genesis, "man" is charged with naming and mastery over land and animals. Terra Nullius, which means "territory without a master" enabled colonizers to lay claim to Indigenous lands (see the definition on the Cornell Law School site, at www.law.cornell.edu/wex/terra_nullius).

6 Quotation from Mother in *Raised by Wolves*, season 1, episode 4 (L. Scott 2020b).

7 Quotation from Mother in *Raised by Wolves*, season 1, episode 2 (R. Scott, 2020b).

8 Though this scene is serene, with Father assuming a pleasant and calming smile, it is similar to what Harrington (2018) describes as "reproductive technohorror" in which "the reproductive female body is compromised, elided or eliminated altogether," and is unsettling in imagining the creation of human babies sans humans (16).

9 A line from the virtual rendering of Campion Sturges in the simulator before his sexual intercourse with Mother (season 1, episode 6 [Mimica-Gezzan 2020b]).

10 In keeping with Mother's metaphor of menopausal transition, while fertility and libido may decline in perimenopause, the rate of unexpected pregnancy is about the same as among younger populations (Baldwin and Jense 2013).

11 This is a line from the virtual Campion Sturges to Mother when sending her on her mission (season 1, episode 5 [Mimica-Gezzan 2020a]).

7. A Long Way from Liberation

1 As a sidenote, it is also worth pointing out that both of these heroines, enabled by the second wave, were depicted by prominent white male directors, a demographic that still dominates Hollywood.

2 As Plant suggests (2010), some of the shifting discourses around motherhood in the past did not translate well outside the confines of the United States. However, as chapter 3 has illustrated in its discussion of HGTV home renovation reality television, international content deals now mean wide circulation of sentiment about mothers steeped in U.S. and Canada culture. Future research could trace whether and how well the idea of maternal angst translates into some of the non-Western territories where these Western media texts circulate widely.

3 Romney (2021) notes that many in the transnational community of the Third World Women's Alliance were part of the second wave, though often forgotten, and colloquially referred to their efforts as "the movement." She also notes that what later became known as second wave feminism was initially known as the "women's movement," gaining serious momentum in August 1970 with the march in support of the national women's strike in New York in which 50,000 people participated.

Works Cited

ABC News. 2012. "Jenny McCarthy on Growing up Poor, Deeply Religious: 'Jesus Was My Bieber.'" *ABC News*, 4 October. https://abcnews.go.com/Entertainment/jenny-mccarthy-growing-poor-deeply-religious-jesus-bieber/story?id=17400887.

Adese, Jennifer. 2022. *Aboriginal™: The Cultural and Economic Politics of Recognition*. Winnipeg: University of Manitoba Press.

Agllias, Kylie. 2011. "No Longer on Speaking Terms: The Losses Associated with Family Estrangement at the End of Life." *Families in Society: The Journal of Contemporary Social Services* 92: 107–13.

Agllias, Kylie. 2013. "The Gendered Experience of Family Estrangement in Later Life." *Affilia: Journal of Women and Social Work* 28, no. 3: 309–21.

Ahmed, Sara. 2010. "Orientations Matter." In *New Materialisms: Ontology, Agency, and Politics*, ed. Diana Coole and Samantha Frost, 234–57. Durham, NC: Duke University Press.

Ahmed, Sara. 2017. *Living a Feminist Life*. Durham, NC: Duke University Press.

Ahmed, Sara. 2023. *The Feminist Killjoy Handbook*. London: Penguin Random House.

Alderman, Liz, and Elian Peltier. 2019. "Roman Polanski Accused of 1975 Rape." *New York Times Online*, 9 November. www.nytimes.com/2019/11/09/world/europe/roman-polanski-rape-france.html.

Alexander-Floyd, Nikol G. 2021. *Re-Imagining Black Women: A Critique of Post-Feminist and Post-Racial Melodrama in Culture and Politics*. New York: NYU Press.

American Psychiatric Association. 2013. "Autism Spectrum Disorder." In *Diagnostic and Statistical Manual of Mental Disorders*. 5th ed. Washington, DC: American Psychiatric Press.

Anderson, Carol. 2016. *White Rage: The Unspoken Truth of Our Racial Divide*. New York: Bloomsbury.

Anderson, Gillian, and Joseph G. Moore. 2014. "Doing It All … and Making It Look Easy!" In *Mothering in the Age of Neoliberalism*, ed. Melinda Vandenbeld Giles, 95–115. Bradford, ON: Demeter Press.

Andrejevic, Mark. 2004. *Reality TV: The Work of Being Watched*. New York: Rowman and Littlefield.

Apprich, Clemens. 2018. "Introduction." In *Pattern Discrimination*, ed. C. Apprich, W. Hui Kyong Chun, F. Cramer, and H. Steyerl, ix–xii. Lüneburg, DE: meson press; Minneapolis: University of Minnesota Press.

Armour, Jody David. 1997. *Negrophobia and Reasonable Racism: The Hidden Costs of Being Black in America*. New York: NYU Press.

Arnold, Sarah. 2013. *Maternal Horror Film: Melodrama and Motherhood*. London: Palgrave Macmillan.

Aspler, John, Kelly D. Harding, and M. Ariel Cascio. 2022. "Representation Matters: Race, Gender, Class, and Intersectional Representations of Autistic and Disabled Characters on Television." *Studies in Social Justice* 16, no. 2: 323–48. https://journals.library.brocku.ca/index.php/SSJ/article/view/2702.

Astrom, Berit. 2017. "Introduction." In *Missing, Presumed Dead: The Absent Mother in the Cultural Imagination*, ed. Astrom Berit, 1–19. London: Palgrave Macmillan.

Baldwin M.K., and J.T. Jensen. 2013. "Contraception during the Perimenopause." *Maturitas* 76, no. 3: 235–42. doi: 10.1016/j.maturitas.2013.07.009.

Barrett, Michele, and Mary McIntosh. 1982. *The Anti-Social Family*. New York: Verso.

Barroso, Amanda, and Juliana Menasce Horowitz. 2021. "The Pandemic Has Highlighted Many Challenges for Mothers, but They Aren't Necessarily New." *Pew Research Centre*, 17 March. www.pewresearch.org/fact-tank/2021/03/17/the-pandemic-has-highlighted-many-challenges-for-mothers-but-they-arent-necessarily-new/.

Barthes, Roland. 1972. *Mythologies*. Translated by A. Lavers. New York: Hill and Wang.

Baudrillard, Jean. 1983. *Simulacra and Simulation*. Los Angeles: Semiotext(e).

BBC. 2018. "Single Mothers 'Hit Hard by Homelessness.'" *BBC News*, 10 October. www.bbc.com/news/uk-45800186.

Belcourt, Billy-Ray. 2014. "Animal Bodies, Colonial Subjects: (Re)Locating Animality in Decolonial Thought." *Societies* 5, no. 1: 1–11.Bennett, Jane. 2010. "A Vitalist Stepover on the Way to New Materialism." In *New*

Materialisms: Ontology, Agency, and Politics, ed. Diana Coole and Samantha Frost, 47–69. Durham, NC: Duke University Press, 47–69.

Berical, Matt. 2021. "What Is the Male Version of a Karen?" Fatherly, 24 May. www.fatherly.com/love-money/male-version-of-karen-meme/.

Berland, Jody. 2009. *North of Empire: Essays on the Cultural Technologies of Space*. Durham, NC: Duke University Press.

The Bible. (1583) 1999. Early English Books Online. Ann Arbor, MI: UMI.

Bjornholt, Margunn. 2020. "Mothering and the Economy." In *The Routledge Companion to Motherhood*, ed. Lynn O'Brien Hallstein, Andrea O'Reilly, and Melinda Vandenbeld Giles, 389–401. New York: Routledge.

Blake, Lucy, Becca Bland, Sarah Foley, and Susan Imrie. 2020. *Family Estrangement and the Covid-19 Crisis*. University of Cambridge Centre for Family Research. www.standalone.org.uk/wp-content/uploads/2020/06/Standalone_Report_v7.pdf.

Blum, Linda M. 2007. "Mother-Blame in the Prozac Nation: Raising Kids with Invisible Disabilities." *Gender and Society* 21, no. 2: 202–26. www.jstor.org/stable/27640959.

Blum, Linda M. 2015. *Raising Generation RX: Mothering Kids with Invisible Disabilities*. New York: NYU Press.

Boss, Pauline. 1999. *Ambiguous Loss: Learning to Live with Unresolved Grief*. Cambridge, MA: Harvard University Press.

Bourdieu, Pierre. 1987. *A Social Critique of the Judgment of Taste*. London: Routledge.

boyd, d., and K. Crawford. 2012. "Critical questions for Big Data: Provocations for a cultural, technological and scholarly phenomenon." *Information, Communication and Society* 15, no. 5: 662–79. https://doi.org/10.1080/1369118X.2012.678878.

Boyer, LeNada. 1997. "Reflections on Alcatraz." In *American Indian Activism: Alcatraz to the Lonest Walk*, ed. Troy Johnson, Joane Nagel, and Duane Champagne, 88–103. Urbana: University of Illinois Press.

Bradley, Laura. 2018. "Modern Family's Big Death Lands with a Whimper." *Vanity Fair*. www.vanityfair.com/hollywood/2018/10/modern-family-death-DeDe-pritchett-shelley-long.

Briggs, Laura. 2018. *How All Politics Became Reproductive Politics: From Welfare Reform to Foreclosure to Trump*. Oakland: University of California Press.

Browne, Simone. 2015. *Dark Matters: On the Surveillance of Blackness*. Durham, NC: Duke University Press.

Brownmiller, Susan. 1975. *Against Our Will*: *Men, Women, and Rape*. New York: Random House.

Bruce, Jean. 2009. "Home Improvement Television: *Holmes on Homes* Makes It Right." *Canadian Journal of Communication* 34, no. 1: 79–94.

Butler, Judith. 1990. *Gender Trouble: Feminism and the Subversion of Identity*. New York: Routledge.

Buzzanell, Patrice M., Robyn V. Remke, Rebecca Meisenbach, Meina Liu, Vanessa Bowers, and Cindy Conn. 2019. "Standpoints of Maternity Leave: Discourses of Temporality and Ability." In *Mothering Rhetorics*, ed. Lynn O'Brien Hallstein, 67–90. New York: Routledge.

Cairns, James. 2017. *The Myth of the Age of Entitlement: Millennials, Austerity, and Hope*. Toronto: University of Toronto Press.

Campbell, Lara, Michael Dawson, and Catherine Gidney. 2022. "Introduction." In *Feeling Feminism: Activism, Affect, and Canada's Second Wave*, ed. Lara Campbell, Michael Dawson, and Catherine Gidney, 3–28. Vancouver: UBC Press.

Canada Mortgage and Housing Corporation (CMHC). 2021a. Homeownership Varies Significantly by Race. Webpage. www.cmhc-schl.gc.ca/en/professionals/housing-markets-data-and-research/housing-research/research-reports/housing-finance/research-insight-homeownership-rate-varies-significantly-race.

Canada Mortgage and Housing Corporation (CMHC). 2021b. Homeownership Varies Significantly by Race. Report. https://assets.cmhc-schl.gc.ca/sites/cmhc/professional/housing-markets-data-and-research/housing-research/research-reports/housing-finance/research-insights/2021/homeownership-rate-varies-significantly-race-en.pdf?rev=af9ae04d-00bd-43ce-8619-d5e5d4a37444.

Cantillon, Sara, and Caitlin McLean. 2016. "Basic Income Guarantee: The Gender Impact within Households." *Journal of Sociology and Social Welfare* 433: 99–120.

Caplan, P.J. 2010. "Mother Blame." In *Encyclopedia of Motherhood*, ed. A. O'Reilly, 94, 803–5. London: Sage Publications.

Capurro, G., J. Greenberg, E. Dube, and M. Driedger. 2018. "Measles, Moral Regulation, and the Social Construction of Risk: Media Narratives of 'Anti-Vaxxers' and the 2015 Disneyland Outbreak." *Canadian Journal of Sociology* 43, no. 1: 25–47. https://doi.org/10.29173/cjs29301.

Caulfield, T., A.R. Marcon, and B. Murdoch. 2017. "Injecting Doubt: Responding to the Naturopathic Anti-Vaccination Rhetoric." *Journal of Law and the Biosciences* 4, no. 2: 229–49. https://doi.org/10.1093/jlb/lsx017.

Centers for Disease Control and Prevention. 2019. Measles Cases and Outbreaks. www.cdc.gov/measles/cases-outbreaks.html.

Centers for Disease Control and Prevention. 2020. Autism and Vaccines. www.cdc.gov/vaccinesafety/concerns/autism.html.

Charmaz, K. 2014. *Constructing Grounded Theory*. 2nd ed. London: Sage Publications.

Cheah, Pheng. 2007. "Biopower and the New International Division of Reproductive Labor." *Boundary 2: An International Journal of Literature and Culture* 341: 90–113.

Christmann, Gabriela B. 2008. "The Power of Photographs of Buildings in the Dresden Urban Discourse: Towards a Visual Discourse Analysis." *Forum Qualitative* 9, no. 3. www.qualitative-research.net/index.php/fqs/article/view/1163/2569.

Clover, Carol. 1992. *Men, Women, and Chain Saws: Gender in the Modern Horror Film*. Princeton, NJ: Princeton University Press.

Cobble, Dorothy Sue. 2004. *The Other Women's Movement: Workplace Justice and Social Rights in Modern America*. Princeton, NJ: Princeton University Press.

Cohen, Cathy J. 2011. "Millennials and the Myth of the Post-Racial Society: Black Youth, Intra-Generational Divisions and the Continuing Racial Divide in American Politics." *Daedalus: Race, Inequality and Culture* 140, no. 2: 197–205.

Cohen, David X., and Matt Groening, exec. producers. 1999–2013. *Futurama* (TV series). Los Angeles: Curiosity Company, 20th Century Fox Television, Fox Television Animation.

Collins, Patricia Hill. 1990. "Mammies, Matriarchs, and Other Controlling Images." In *Black Feminist Thought: Knowledge, Consciousness, and the Politics of Empowerment*, 76–106. Routledge: New York.

Collins, Patricia Hill. 1994. "Shifting the Center: Race, Class, and Feminist Theorising about Motherhood." In *Mothering: Ideology, Experience, and Agency*, ed. Evelyn Nagano Glenn, Grace Chang, and Linda Reddie Forcey, 45–65. New York: Routledge.

Combahee River Collective. (1977) 2017. "The Combahee River Collective Statement." In *How We Get Free: Black Feminism and the Combahee River Collective*, ed. Keeanga-Yamahtta Taylor, 15–28. Chicago: Haymarket Books.

Conti, Richard P. 2015. "Family Estrangement: Establishing a Prevalence Rate." *Psychology* 3, no. 2: 2374–99.

Coole, Diana, and Samantha Frost. 2010. "Introduction." In *New Materialisms: Ontology, Agency, and Politics*, ed. Diana Coole and Samantha Frost. Durham, NC: Duke University Press, 1–43.

Corus. 2022. "TV That Feels Like Home: Corus Entertainment Welcomes Chip and Joanna Gaines' Magnolia Network to Canada March 28." Magnolia Network / Corus press release, 1 March.

https://assets.corusent.com/wp-content/uploads/2022/02/Magnolia
-Network-Launch-Press-Release.pdf.

Couldry, Nick. 2012. *Media, Society, World: Social Theory and Digital Media Practice.* Cambridge: Polity Press.

Couthard, Glen Sean. 2014. *Red Skins, White Masks: Rejecting the Colonial Politics of Recognition.* Minneapolis: University of Minnesota Press.

Creed, Barbara. 1993. *The Monstrous-Feminine: Film, Feminism, Psychoanalysis.* London: Routledge.

Dalla Costa, Mariarosa. (1972) 2016. "Women and the Subversion of the Community." In *Revolutionary Feminism: Communist Interventions,* 3:, 237–88. New York: Communist Research Cluster. https://communistresearchcluster .files.wordpress.com/2016/04/crc_ci_vol_three_2_01.pdf.

Daniels, G., R. Gervais, S. Merchant, H. Klein, K. Kwapis, J. Lieberstein, B.J. Novak, M. Kaling, B. Forrester, and D. Sterling, exec. producers. 2005–13. *The Office* (TV series). Reveille Productions NBC Universal Television 3 Arts Entertainment.

Darby, Seyward. 2020. *Sisters in Hate: American Women on the Front Lines of White Nationalism.* New York: Little, Brown.

David, Daryn H., Lillian Gelberg, and Nancy E. Suchman. 2012. "Implications of Homelessness for Parenting Young Children: A Preliminary Review from a Developmental Attachment Perspective." *Infant Mental Health Journal* 33, no. 1: 1–9.

Davis, Angela. 1981. "The Approaching Obsolescence." In *Women, Race and Class.* New York: Random House.

Dawkins, R. (1976) 1989. *The Selfish Gene.* Oxford: Oxford University Press.

Dekel, Jon. 2015. "How a Canadian Couple Discovered the American Dream in Nashville." *National Post,* 26 May. https://nationalpost.com /entertainment/television/how-a-canadian-couple-discovered-the -american-dream-in-nashville.

Deloria Jr., Vine. (1973) 2003. *God Is Red: A Native View of Religion.* 30th anniversary ed. Wheat Ridge, Colorado: Fulcrum Publishing.

DiAngelo, Robin. 2018. *White Fragility: Why Understanding Racism Can Be So Hard for White People.* Boston: Beacon Press.

Dobson, K., and I. Knezevic. 2017. "'Liking and Sharing': The Stigmatization of Poverty and Social Welfare through Internet Memes on Social Media." *tripleC: Communication, Capitalism and Critique* 15, no. 2: 777–95. https:// doi.org/10.31269/triplec.v15i2.815.

Douglas, Patty, and Estee Klar. 2020. *Beyond Disordered Brains and Mother Blame: Critical Issues in Autism and Mothering.* New York: Routledge.

Draper, Nora. 2019. *The Identity Trade: Selling Privacy and Reputation Online.* New York: NYU Press.

Drozd, L.M., and N.W. Olesen. 2004. "Is It Abuse, Alienation, and/or Estrangement?" *Journal of Child Custody* 1: 65–106.

Dubrofsky, Rachel E. 2022. *Authenticating Whiteness: Karens, Selfies, and Pop Stars*. Jackson: University Press of Mississippi.

Duffy, Mignon. 2007. "Doing the Dirty Work: Gender, Race, and Reproductive Labour in Historical Perspective." *Gender and Society* 21, no. 3: 313–36.

Dunbar, Roxanne. (1969) 2016. "Female Liberation as the Basis for Social Revolution." In *Revolutionary Feminism: Communist Interventions*, 3: 148–50. New York: Communist Research Cluster. https://communistresearchcluster .files.wordpress.com/2016/04/crc_ci_vol_three_2_01.pdf.

Durbach, N. 2005. *Bodily Matters: The Anti-Vaccination Movement in England, 1853–1907*. Durham, NC: Duke University Press.

Dyer, Richard. 2005. "The Matter of Whiteness." In *White Privilege: Essential Readings*, ed. Paula Rothenberg, 9–14. New York: Worth Publishers.

Dyer, Richard. 2017. *White*. 20th anniversary ed. New York: Routledge.

Echols, Alice. 2002. *Shaky Ground: The Sixties and Its Aftershocks*. New York: Columbia University Press.

Edwards, Allison. (1976) 2016. "Rape, Racism, and the White Women's Movement." In *Revolutionary Feminism: Communist Interventions*, 3: 226–37. New York: Communist Research Cluster. https://communistresearchcluster .files.wordpress.com/2016/04/crc_ci_vol_three_2_01.pdf.

Ehrenreich, Barbara, and Deirdre English. 1978. *For Her Own Good: Two Centuries of the Experts' Advice to Women*. New York: Anchor Books.

Emmons, L. 2020. "Central Park Karen Busted – but She's Suffered Enough." *New York Post*, 6 July. https://nypost.com/2020/07/06/central-park -karen-busted-but-shes-suffered-enough/.

Engels, Friedrich. (1884) 2016. "Origins of the Family, Private Property, and the State." In *Revolutionary Feminism: Communist Interventions*, 3:, 1–32. New York: Communist Research Cluster. https:// communistresearchcluster.files.wordpress.com/2016/04/crc_ci_vol _three_2_01.pdf.

Essman, Scott. 2020. "The Production Design on *Raised by Wolves*." *Below the Line*, 14 October. www.btlnews.com/featured/raised-by-wolves/.

Eyrenci, Duygu. 2013. "*Rosemary's Baby* (1986) USA Director Roman Polanski." *Film Matters* 4, no. 1: 73. doi:10.1386/fm.4.1.73_1.

Fanon, Frantz. (1952) 2008. *Black Skins, White Masks*. Translated by Richard Philcox. New York: Grove Press.

Federici, Silvia. (1975) 2020a. "Counterplanning from the Kitchen." In *Revolution at Point Zero: Housework, Reproduction, and Feminist Struggle*, 24–36. New York: PM Press.

Federici, Silvia. (1975) 2020b. "Wages against Housework." In *Revolution at Point Zero: Housework, Reproduction, and Feminist Struggle*, 11–18. New York: PM Press.

Federici, Silvia. (1975) 2020c. "Why Sexuality Is Work." In *Revolution at Point Zero: Housework, Reproduction, and Feminist Struggle*, 19–23. New York: PM Press.

Federici, Silvia. 2004. *Caliban and the Witch: Women, the Body, and Primitive Accumulation*. New York: Autonomedia.

Federici, Silvia. 2020. *Revolution at Point Zero: Housework, Reproduction, and Feminist Struggle*. Oakland: PM Press.

Federici, Silvia, and Arlen Austin, eds. 2017. *Wages for Housework: The New York Committee, 1972–1977. History, Theory, Documents*. Brooklyn: Autonomedia.

Feldstein, Ruth. 2000. *Motherhood in Black and White: Race and Sex in American Liberalism, 1930–1965*. Ithaca, NY: Cornell University Press.

Firestone, Shulamith. 1970. *The Dialectic of Sex: The Case for Feminist Revolution*. New York: William Morrow and Company.

Firestone, Shulamith, and Anne Koedt. [1968] 2016. "Redstockings Manifesto." In *Revolutionary Feminism: Communist Interventions*, 3: 143–4. New York: Communist Research Cluster. Accessed 13 September 2021. https://communistresearchcluster.files.wordpress.com/2016/04/crc_ci _vol_three_2_01.pdf.

Fisher, B.L., and H.L. Coulter. 2002. *A Shot in the Dark*. Westminster: Penguin.

Fischer-Tiné, Harald. 2016. *Anxieties, Fear, and Panic in Colonial Settings: Empires on the Verge of a Nervous Breakdown*. Houndmills, UK: Palgrave Macmillan.

Fiske, J. 1989. *Reading the Popular*. Boston: Unwin Hyman.

Foertsch, Jacqueline. 2019. "Tools of the Trade: Working Women in Texts from the Sexual Revolution." *CEA Critic* 81, no. 2: 100–16. doi:10.1353/cea.2019.0015.

Forbes, Bryan, dir. 1975. *The Stepford Wives*. Los Angeles: Palomar Pictures International.

Foucault, Michel. 1972. *The Archaeology of Knowledge and the Discourse on Language*. New York: Pantheon.

Foucault, Michel. 1977. *Discipline and Punish*. London: Tavistock.

Foucault, Michel. 1980. *Power/Knowledge*. Brighton: Harvester.

Foucault, Michel. 1982. "The Subject and Power." In *Beyond Structuralism and Hermeneutics*, ed. H. Dreyfus and P. Rabinow, 208–26. Brighton, UK: Harvester.

Foundation Marketing. (2021). Reddit Statistics 2021: Demographics, usage and traffic data. Available at: https://foundationinc.co/lab/reddit -statistics/.

Friedan, Betty. 1963. *The Feminine Mystique*. New York: W.W. Norton.

Friedman, May, and Emily Satterthwaite. 2021. "Same Storm, Different Boats: Some Thoughts on Gender, Race, and Class in the Time of COVID-19." In *Mothers, Mothering, and COVID-19*, ed. Andrea O'Reilly and Fiona Joy Green, 53–63. Bradford, ON: Demeter Press.

Fritsch, Kelly. 2015. "Desiring Disability Differently: Neoliberalism, Heterotopic Imagination and Intra-Corporeal Reconfigurations." *Foucault Studies* 19: 43–66.

Garcia, Leonardo Adrian, and Chris O'Falt. 2021. "*Raised by Wolves*: Artisans Discuss Creating Ridley Scott's Latest Sci-i Dystopia." *IndieWire*, 16 February. www.indiewire.com/video/raised-by-wolves-creating-ridley -scott-sci-fi-dystopia-1234617239/.

Gee, Sarah, and Steven Jackson. 2017. "Screening Masculinity: Crisis, Promotional Culture, Consumption, and Sport." In *Sport, Promotional Culture, and the Crisis of Masculinity*, 57–90. UK: Palgrave Macmillan.

Gill, Rosalind. 2007. "Postfeminism: Elements of a Sensibility." *European Journal of Cultural Studies* 10, no. 2: 147–66. doi:10.1177/ 1367549407075898.

Gilligan, Carol. 1982. *In a Different Voice: Psychological Theory and Women's Development*. Cambridge, MA: Harvard University Press.

Goldberg, Jonathan. 2004. *Tempest in the Caribbean*. Minneapolis: University of Minnesota Press.

Gordon, Avery F. (1997) 2008. *Ghostly Matters: Haunting and the Sociological Imagination*. Minneapolis: University of Minnesota Press.

Gordon, Linda. 2013. "Socialist Feminism: The Legacy of the 'Second Wave.'" *New Labour Forum* 22, no. 3: 20–8.

Grande, Laura. 2019. "7 Things You Didn't Know about *Masters of Flip*'s Dave Wilson." HGTV, 17 May. www.hgtv.ca/things-you-didnt-know -masters-of-flip-dave-wilson/.

Greenslade, Frances, ed. 2017. *Absent Mothers*. Bradford, ON: Demeter Press.

Gries, L. 2015. *Still Life with Rhetoric: A New Materialist Approach for Visual Rhetorics*. Logan: Utah State University Press.

Hall, Stuart. (1973) 1991. "Encoding/Decoding." In *The Cultural Studies Reader*, ed. S. During, 90–103. London: Routledge.

Hall, Stuart. 1997. *Representation: Cultural Representations and Signifying Practices*, ed. Stuart Hall, London: Sage Publications.

Harrell, Zaje A.T. 2021. "And Then We Went Outside: A Black Mothering Lens on Quarantine, Health Disparities, and State Violence." In *Mothers, Mothering, and COVID-19*, ed. Andrea O'Reilly and Fiona Joy Green, 329–40. Bradford, ON: Demeter Press.

Harrington, Erin. 2018. *Gynaehorror: Women, Monstrosity and Horror Film.* London: Routledge.

Hawkins, D. 2020. "Disparities in the Usage of Maternity Leave According to Occupation, Race/Ethnicity, and Education." *American Journal of Industrial Medicine*, 63, no. 12: 1134–44.

Hayden, Casey, and Mary King. (1965) 2016. "Sex and Cast." In *Revolutionary Feminism: Communist Interventions*, 3: 141–2. New York: Communist Research Cluster. https://communistresearchcluster.files.wordpress .com/2016/04/crc_ci_vol_three_2_01.pdf.

Hays, Sharon. 1998. *The Cultural Contradictions of Motherhood.* New Haven, CT: Yale University Press.

Hearn, Alison. 2009. "Insecure: Narratives and Economies of the Branded Self in Transformation Television." In *TV Transformations: Revealing the Makeover Show*, ed. Tanya Lewis, 55–64. New York: Routledge.

Henaway, Mostafa. 2023. *Essential Work, Disposable Workers.* Halifax: Fernwood.

Hennessy, Rosemary, and Chrys Ingraham. 1997. "Introduction." In *Materialist Feminism: A Reader in Class, Difference, and Women's Lives*, ed. Rosemary Hennessy and Chrys Ingraham, 1–16. New York: Routledge.

Hess, Megan. 2016. "Second and Third-Wave Feminist Values and Culture in the Stepford Wives." Cinemablography, 22 November. www.cinemablography .org/blog/second-and-third-wave-feminist-values-and-culture-in-the -stepford-wives.

Hills, T.T. 2019. "The Dark Side of Information Proliferation." *Perspectives on Psychological Science* 14, no. 3: 323–30. https://doi .org/10.1177/1745691618803647.

hooks, bell. (1981) 2015. *Ain't I a Woman? Black Women and Feminism.* London: Routledge.

Howard, Byron, and Jared Bush, dirs. 2021. *Encanto* (animated film). Burbank, CA: Walt Disney Animation Studios.

Hviid, A., J.V. Hansen, M. Frisch, and M. Melbye. 2019. "Measles, Mumps, Rubella Vaccination and Autism." *Annals of Internal Medicine* 170, no. 8: 513–20. https://doi.org/10.7326/M18-2101.

IMDb. 2022. "Amanda Collin." www.imdb.com/name/nm4518657/.

Jack, Jordynn. 2014. *Autism and Gender: From Refrigerator Mothers to Computer Geeks.* Urbana: University of Illinois Press.

James, Selma. (1952) 2012. "A Woman's Place." In *Sex, Race, and Class: The Perspective of Winning: A Selection of Writings, 1952–2011*, 13–31. Oakland: PM Press.

James, Selma. (1972) 2012. "The Power of Women and the Subversion of Community." In *Sex, Race, and Class: The Perspective of Winning: A Selection of Writings, 1952–2011*, 43–59. Oakland: PM Press.

James, Selma. (1973) 2012. "The Perspective of Winning." In *Sex, Race, and Class: The Perspective of Winning: A Selection of Writings, 1952–2011*, 76–85. Oakland: PM Press.

James, Selma. (1975) 2012. "Wageless of the World." In *Sex, Race, and Class: The Perspective of Winning: A Selection of Writings, 1952–2011*, 102–8. Oakland: PM Press.

James, Selma. (1983) 2012. "Marx and Feminism." In *Sex, Race, and Class: The Perspective of Winning: A selection of Writings 1952–2011*, 141–60. Oakland: PM Press.

James, Selma. 2012. *Sex, Race, and Class: The Perspective of Winning. A Selection of Writings, 1952–2011*. Oakland: PM Press.

Kampel, Stewart. 2007. "Levin, Ira." *Encyclopedia Judaica*, vol. 12, ed. Michael Barenbaum and Fred Skoinik. Farmington Hills: Macmillan Reference. Gael eBooks.

Kata, A. 2012. "Antivaccine Activists, Web 2.0, and the Postmodern Paradigm: An Overview of Tactics and Tropes Used Online by the Anti-Vaccination Movement." *Elsevier* 30, no. 25: 3778–89. doi: 10.1016/j.vaccine.2011.11.112.

Kelly, Joan B., and Johnston, Janet R. 2001. "The Alienated Child: A Reformulation of Parental Alienation Syndrome." *Family Court Review* 39, no. 3: 249–66. https://doi.org/10.1111/j.174-1617.2001.tb00609.x.

Kelly, Joan B., and Johnston, Janet R. 2004. "Rejoinder to Gardner's Commentary on Kelly and Johnston's 'The Alienated Child: A Reformulation of Parental Alienation Syndrome.'" *Family Court Review* 42, no. 4: 622–8. https://doi.org/10.1111/j.174-1617.2004.tb01328.x.

Kelly, M. 2019. "Twitter Fights Vaccine Misinformation with New Search Tool. *The Verge*. 14 May. www.theverge.com/2019/5/14/18623494/twitter-vaccine-misinformation-anti-vax-search-tool-instagram-facebook.

Kennedy, Tanya Ann. 2017. *Historicizing Post-Discourses: Postfeminism and Postracialism in United States Culture*. New York: SUNY Press.

King, Samantha. 2008. *Pink Ribbons Inc.: Breast Cancer and the Politics of Philanthropy*. Minneapolis: University of Minnesota Press.

King, Wendy C., Max Rubinstein, Alex Reinhart, and Robin Mejia. 2021. "Time Trends, Factors Associated with, and Reasons for COVID-19 Vaccine Hesitancy: A Massive Online Survey of US Adults from January–May 2021." *PLoS ONE* 16, no. 12: e0260731. https://doi.org/10.1371/journal.pone.0260731.

Kolodiejzyk, C. 2018. Karen. *ifunny*. 18 March. https://ifunny.co
/picture/karen-44-mother-of-three-blonde-owns-a-volvo-annoying
-M1jVTNFp6.

Kretschmer, Kelsy. 2019. *Fighting for NOW: Diversity and Discord in the National Organization for Women*. Minneapolis: University of Minnesota Press.

Kristeva, Julia. 1982. *Powers of Horror: An Essay on Abjection*. New York: Columbia University Press.

Kynard, Carmen. 2012. "'Beyond Miranda's Meaning': My First Two Lessons." *Education, Liberation, and Black Radical Traditions for the 21st Century* (blog). http://carmenkynard.org/beyond-mirandas
-meanings/.

Ladd-Taylor, M., and Umansky, L. eds. 1998. *"Bad" Mothers: The Politics of Blame in Twentieth-Century America*. New York: NYU Press.

LaDuke, Winona. 1982. *All Our Relations: Native Struggles for Land and Life*. Boston: South End Press.

Laslett, Barbara, and Johanna Brenner. 1989. "Gender and Social Reproduction: Historical Perspectives." *Annual Review of Sociology* 15: 381–404.

Lau, T.C.W. 2016. "Representing Anti-Vaccination: From James Gillray to Jenny McCarthy." *InVisible Culture: An Electronic Journal for Visual Culture*. 22 January. https://ivc.lib.rochester.edu/representing-anti-vaccination
-from-james-gillray-to-jenny-mccarthy/.

Levin, Ira. (1967) 2017. *Rosemary's Baby*. New York: Pegasus Books.

Levin, Ira. (1972) 1998. *The Stepford Wives*. New York: William Morrow.

Lewis, Jane. 2006. "The Adult Worker Model: Family, Care, and the Problem of Gender Equality." *Journal of Poverty and Social Justice* 1, no. 1: 33–8.

Lewis, Sophie. 2019. *Full Surrogacy Now: Feminism against Family*. London: Verso Books.

Lewis, Tanya, ed. 2009. *TV Transformations: Revealing the Makeover Show*. New York: Routledge.

Little, Lora C. 2013. "Be Your Own Doctor." *Morning Oregonian*, 14 October, 15.

Littler, Jo. 2020. "Mothers Behaving Badly: Chaotic Hedonism and the Crisis of Neoliberal Social Reproduction." *Cultural Studies* 34, no. 4: 499–520.

Livingston, Gretchen, and Deja Thomas. 2019. "Among 41 Countries, Only US Lacks Paid Parental Leave." *Pew Research Centre*. 16 December. www
.pewresearch.org/fact-tank/2019/12/16/u-s-lacks-mandated-paid
-parental-leave/.

Louisias, Margee, and Lyndonna Marrast. 2020. "Intersectional Identity and Racial Inequality during the COVID-19 Pandemic: Perspectives of Black Physician Mothers." *Journal of Women's Health* 29, no. 9: 1148–9. doi: 10.1089/jwh.2020.8677.

Lunt, Peter. 2008. "Little Angels: The Mediation of Parenting." *Continuum: Journal of Media and Cultural Studies* 22: 537–46. https://bura.brunel .ac.uk/bitstream/2438/4249/1/Fulltext.pdf.

Major, Darren. 2021. "Indigenous Women Make Up Almost Half the Female Prison Population, Ombudsman Says." *CBC*. 18 December. www.cbc.ca /news/politics/indigenous-women-half-inmate-population-canada-1.6289674.

Majumder, Maimuna S., Emily L. Cohn, Sumiko R. Mekaru, et al. 2015. "Substandard Vaccination Compliance and the 2015 Measles Outbreak." *JAMA Pediatrics* 169: 494–5. 10.1001/jamapediatrics.2015.0384.

Markham, Annette. 2016. "OK Cupid Data Release Fiasco: It's Time to Rethink Ethics Education." AnnetteMarkham. 19 May. https:// annettemarkham.com/2016/05/okcupid-data-release-fiasco-its-time-to -rethink-ethics-education/.

Marx, Karl. (1867) 1977. *Capital*, vol. 1. New York: Vintage Books.

McCarthy, Jenny. 2008. *Mother Warriors: A Nation of Parents Healing Autism against All Odds*. Dutton Adult.

McGuire, A. 2016. *War on Autism: On the Cultural Logics of Normative Violence*. University of Michigan Press.

McKay, Alisa. 2001. "Rethinking Work and Income Maintenance Policy: Promoting Gender Equality through a Citizens' Basic Income." *Feminist Economics* 7, no. 1: 97–118.

McKittrick, Katherine. 2006. *Demonic Grounds: Black Women and the Cartographies of Struggle*. Minneapolis: University of Minnesota Press.

McKittrick, Katherine. 2021. *Dear Science and Other Stories*. Durham, NC: Duke University Press.

McLuhan, Marshall. (1964) 2001. *Understanding Media: The Extensions of Man*. Oxford: Taylor and Francis.

McRobbie, Angela. 2000. *Feminism and Youth Culture*. New York: Routledge.

McRobbie, Angela. 2020. *Feminism and the Politics of Resilience: Essays on Gender, Media, and the End of Welfare*. Cambridge: UK: Polity Press.

Meek, Andy. 2021. "New Season of a Smash-Hit Show Has Netflix Viewers Glued to Their Screen." *BGR*. 13 October. https://bgr.com /entertainment/new-season-of-a-smash-hit-show-has-netflix-viewers -glued-to-their-screens/.

Meredith Corporation. 2022. Magnolia Journal Media Kit. www.meredith .com/Magnolia-Journal-Media-Kit.pdf.

Milner, Ryan M. 2013. "FCJ-156 Hacking the Social: Internet Memes, Identity Antagonism, and the Logic of Lulz." *Fibreculture Journal* 22: 62–92.

Milton, Damien. 2020. "Neurodiversity Past and Present: An Introduction to the Neurodiversity Movement." In *The Neurodiversity Reader: Exploring*

Concepts, Lived Experience, and Implications for Practice, ed. Damian Milton, 3–6. West Sussex, UK: Pavilion.

Milton, John. (1667) 1998. *Paradise Lost*. London: Longman.

Miranda, Lin-Manuel. 2021. "We Don't Talk about Bruno." (Song in *Encanto*). Burbank, CA: Walt Disney Animation Studios.

Moore, Kasey. 2020. "Series That Dominated Netflix Top 10s in 2020." What's on Netflix. 28 December. www.whats-on-netflix.com/what-to-watch /series-that-dominated-the-netflix-top-10s-in-2020/.

Moreton-Robinson, Aileen. (2000) 2020. *Talkin' Up to the White Woman*. Minneapolis: University of Minnesota Press.

Morse, Anne. 2022. "Stable Fertility Rates 1990–2019 Mask Distinct Variations by Age." United States Census Bureau. 6 April. www.census .gov/library/stories/2022/04/fertility-rates-declined-for-younger -women-increased-for-older-women.html.

Moseley, Rachel, Tanya Druce, and Julie Turner-Cobb. 2020. "'When My Autism Broke': A Qualitative Study Spotlighting Autistic Voices on Menopause." *Autism* 24, no. 6: 1423–37.

Motrescu-Mayes, Annamaria, and Susan Aasman. 2019. *Amateur Media and Participatory Cultures: Film, Video, and Digital Media*. London: Routledge.

Moyser, Melissa. 2017. "Women and Paid Work." Statistics Canada. https:// www150.statcan.gc.ca/n1/pub/89-503-x/2015001/article/14694-eng.htm.

Moyser, Melissa, and Amanda Burlock. 2018. "Time Use: Total Work Burden, Unpaid Work, and Leisure." In *Women in Canada: A Gender-Based Statistical Report*, 7th ed., 489–503. Ottawa: Statistics Canada.

Munn, James, and Bob Willoughby. 2018. *This Is No Dream: The Making of Rosemary's Baby*. London: Reel Art Press.

Munro, Ealasaid. 2013. "Feminism: A Fourth Wave?" *Political Insight* 4: 22–5.

Nagesh, A. 2020. "What Exactly Is a Karen and Where Did the Meme Come From?" *BBC News*. 31 July. www.bbc.com/news/world-53588201.

National Inquiry into Murdered and Missing Indigenous Women and Girls. 2019. *Reclaiming Power and Place: The Final Report of the National Inquiry into Missing and Murdered Indigenous Women and Girls*. www.mmiwg -ffada.ca/final-report/.

National Institute for Health and Care Excellence. (2015) 2019. "Menopause: Diagnosis and Management." www.nice.org.uk/guidance/ng23.

Netflix. 2021. "Top 10 by Country." 17 October. Netflix. https://top10.netflix .com/tv/2021-10-17.

Nguyen, K.H., Srivastav, A., Razzaghi, H., Williams, W., Lindley, M.C., Jorgensen, C., Neetu, A., Singleton, J.A. 2021. "COVID-19 Vaccination Intent, Perceptions, and Reasons for Not Vaccinating among Groups Prioritized for Early Vaccination: United States, September and December

2020." *Morbidity and Mortality Weekly Report* 70, no. 6: 217–22. http://dx
.doi.org/10.15585/mmwr.mm7006e3external icon.

Nicholls, Larissa, and Yolanda Stengers. 2019. "Robotic Vacuum Cleaners
Save Energy? Raising Cleanliness Conventions and Energy Demand in
Australian Households with Smart Home Technologies." *Energy Research
and Social Science* 50: 73–81.

O'Brien Hallstein, Lynn. 2016. *Bikini Ready Moms: Celebrity Profiles,
Motherhood, and the Body.* New York: State University of New York Press.

OECD. 2011. *Doing Better for Families.* https://web-archive.oecd.org/2014
-08-21/60776-doingbetterforfamilies.htm.

Oliver, M. 2013. "The Social Model of Disability: Thirty Years On." *Disability and
Society* 28, no. 7: 1024–6. https://doi.org/10.1080/09687599.2013.818773.

O'Reilly, Andrea. 2020. "Matricentric Feminism." In *The Routledge Companion
to Motherhood*, ed. Lynn O'Brien Hallstein, Andrea O'Reilly, and Melinda
Vandenbeld Giles, 51–60. London: Routledge.

O'Reilly, Andrea. 2021. *Matricentric Feminism: Theory, Activism, Practice*, 2nd
ed. Bradford, ON: Demeter Press.

O'Reilly, Andrea, ed. 2023. *Normative Motherhood: Regulations, Representations,
and Regulations.* Bradford, ON: Demeter Press.

Ouellette, Laurie, and James Hay. 2008. *Better Living through Reality TV:
Television and Post-Welfare Citizenship.* Malden, MA: Blackwell Publishing.

Panek, E.T. 2022. *Understanding Reddit.* London: Routledge.

Patel, M., A.D. Lee, N.S. Clemmons, et al. 2019. "National Update on
Measles Cases and Outbreaks: United States, January 1–October 1, 2019."
Morbidity and Mortality Weekly Report 68, no. 40: 893–6. http://dx.doi.org
/10.15585/mmwr.mm6840e2external icon.

Petersen, Anne Helen. 2019. "'Fixer Upper' Is Over, but Waco's
Transformation Is Just Beginning." *BuzzFeedNews.* 20 April. www
.buzzfeednews.com/article/annehelenpetersen/waco-texas-magnolia
-fixer-upper-antioch-chip-joanna-gaines.

Pillemer, Karl. 2020. *Fault Lines: Fractured Families and How to Mend Them.*
New York: Avery.

Pizzorno, Joseph. 2018. "Environmental Toxins and Infertility." *Integrative
Medicine (Encinitas)* 17, no. 2: 8–11. https://www.ncbi.nlm.nih.gov/pmc
/articles/PMC6396757/.

Plant, Rebecca Jo. 2010. *Mom: The Transformation of Motherhood in Modern
America.* Chicago: University of Chicago Press.

Polanski, Roman, dir. 1968. *Rosemary's Baby.* Los Angeles: William Castle
Productions.

PR Newswire. 2016. "Corus Entertainment Announces Multiple New
International Content Deals for Original Series Buying the View, Masters

of Flip, and Cheer Squad." 19 September. www.prnewswire.com/news
-releases/corus-entertainment-announces-multiple-new-international
-content-deals-for-original-series-buying-the-view-masters-of-flip-and
-cheer-squad-593999831.html.

PR Newswire. 2017. "Corus Studios Announces New Sales for Its Original
Content Ahead of MIPCOM." 11 October. www.newswire.ca/news
-releases/corus-studios-announces-new-sales-for-its-original-content
-ahead-of-mipcom-650498813.html.

Press, Andrea L., and Francesca Tripodi. 2021. *Media-Ready Feminism and
Everyday Sexism: How US Audiences Create Meaning across Platforms*. New
York: SUNY Press.

Prince. 2007. "F.U.N.K." NPG Digital.

Ray, Rashawn. 9 April 2020. "Why Are Blacks Dying at Higher Rates from
COVID-19?" *Brooking*, 9 April. https://www.brookings.edu/articles
/why-are-blacks-dying-at-higher-rates-from-covid-19/.

Reagan, Leslie. 1997. *When Abortion Was a Crime: Women, Medicine, and Law
in the United States*. Berkeley and Los Angeles: University of California
Press.

Rich, Adrienne. 1976. *Of Women Born: Motherhood as Experience and Institution*.
New York: W.W. Norton.

Richardson, Brooke. 2020. "Shifting Gender Roles and Childcare in Canada." In
The Routledge Companion to Motherhood, ed. Lynn O'Brien Hallstein, Andrea
O'Reilly, and Melinda Vandenbeld Giles, 353–61. New York: Routledge.

Rivers, Nichola. 2017. *Postfeminism(s) and the Arrival of the Fourth Wave:
Turning Tides*. Camden, UK: Palgrave.

Romano, A. 2020. "Karen: The Anti-Vaxxer Soccer Mom with Speak-to-the
-Manager Hair, Explained." *Vox*. 5 February. www.vox.com/2020/2/5
/21079162/karen-name-insult-meme-manager.

Romney, Patricia. 2021. *We Were There: The Third World Women's Alliance and
the Second Wave*. New York: Feminist Press at CUNY.

Rosenberg, Buck Clifford. 2011. "Domestic Taste, DIY, and the Property
Market, Home Cultures, Home Improvement." *Home Cultures: The Journal
of Architecture, Design and Domestic Space* 8, no. 1: 5–23. doi: 10.2752/17517
4211X12863597046578.

Ryan, Kennedy Laborde. 2022. "Stim, Like, and Subscribe: Autistic Children
and Family YouTube Channels." *Studies in Social Justice* 16, no. 2. doi:
https://doi.org/10.26522/ssj.v16i2.2650.

Ryan, Rebecca M. 1995. "The Sex Right: A Legal History of the Marital Rape
Exemption." *Law and Social Inquiry* 20, no. 4: 941–1001.

Said, Edward W. 1993. *Culture and Imperialism*. London: Vintage.

Samhan, Jamie. 2019. "'Masters of Flip' Co-hosts Kortney and Dave Wilson Divorcing." *Global News*. 20 December. https://globalnews .ca/news/6321499/masters-of-flip-hosts-kortney-and-dave-wilson -divorcing/.

Scharp, Kristina M., and Elizabeth Dorrance Hall. 2017. "Family Marginalization, Alienation, and Estrangement: Questioning the Nonvoluntary Status of Family Relationships." *Annals of the International Communication Association* 41, no. 1: 28–45.

Schmidt, Mackenzie. 2021. "Syd and Shae McGee Nearly Went Broke before 'Dream Home Makeover': 'There Wasn't a Backup Plan.'" *People*. 20 January. https://people.com/home/dream-home-makeovers-syd -and-shea-mcgee-nearly-went-broke-before-finding-fame-there-wasnt-a -backup-plan/.

Schoppe-Sullivan, S.J., J. Coleman, J. Wang, and J.J. Yan. 2021. "Mothers' Attributions for Estrangement from Their Adult Children." *Couple and Family Psychology: Research and Practice* 12, no. 3: 146–54. https://doi .org/10.1037/cfp0000198.

Scott, Mark. 2022. "Ottawa Truckers Convoy Galvanizes Far Right World-Wide." *Politico*. 6 February. www.politico.com/news/2022/02/06 /ottawa-truckers-convoy-galvanizes-far-right-worldwide-00006080.

Scott, Ridley, dir. 1979. *Alien*. Los Angeles: 20th Century Fox.

Scott, Ridley, dir. 1982. *Bladerunner*. Hollywood: The Lad Company Shaw Brothers Blade Runner Partnership.

Scott, Ridley, dir. 2012. *Prometheus*. Hollywood and London: 20th Century Studios and Scott Free Productions.

Sedinova, Hana. 2016. "The 'Lamia" and Aristotle's Beaver: The Consequences of a Mistranscription." *Journal of the Warburg and Courtauld Institutes* 79: 295–306.

Segev, E., A. Nissenbaum, N. Stolero, and L. Shifman. 2015. "Families and Networks of Internet Memes: The Relationship between Cohesiveness, Uniqueness, and Quiddity Concreteness." *Journal of Computer-Mediated Communication*, 20, no. 4: 417–33. https://doi.org/10.1111/jcc4.12120.

Sender, Katherine. 2006. "Queens for a Day: Queer Eye for the Straight Guy and the Neoliberal Project." *Critical Studies in Media Communication* 23, no. 2: 131–51.

Shakespeare, William. ([Ca. 1610] 1995. *The Tempest*. Buckingham, UK: Open University Press.

Sharma, Sarah. 2022. "Introduction." In *Re-Understanding Media: Feminist Extensions of Marshall McLuhan*, ed. Sarah Sharma and Rianka Singh, 1–19. Durham, NC: Duke University Press.

Shaw, Ted. 2009. "Meet the Wilsons: CMT Reality Stars." *CanWestNews*, 18 September.

Shelley, Mary Wollstonecraft. (1818) 1999. *Frankenstein, or, the Modern Prometheus*. Peterborough, ON: Broadview Press.

Shifman, L. 2013. *Memes in Digital Culture*. Cambridge, MA: MIT Press.

Short, Sue. 2007. *Misfit Sisters: Screen Horror as Female Rites of Passage*. UK: Palgrave Macmillan.

Simpson, Leanne Betasamosake. 2011. *Dancing on Our Turtle's Back: Stories of Nishnaabeg Re-Creation*. Winnipeg: Arbeiter Ring Publishing.

Singh, Rianka, and Sarah Sharma. 2019. "Platform Uncommons." *Feminist Media Studies* 19, no. 2: 302–3.

Skeggs, Beverly. 2009. "The Moral Economy of Person Production: Class Relations of Self-Performance on 'Reality' Television." *Sociological Review* 54, no. 4: 626–44.

Sobchack, Vivian. (1996) 2015. "Bringing It All Back Home: Family Economy and Generic Exchange." In *The Dread of Difference: Gender and the Horror Film*, ed. Barry Keith Grant, 2nd ed., 171–91. Austin: University of Texas Press.

Sousa, A. 2011. "From Refrigerator Mothers to Warrior-Heroes: The Cultural Identity Transformation of Mothers Raising Children with Intellectual Disabilities." *Symbolic Interaction* 34, no. 2: 220–43. https://doi.org/10.1525/si.2011.34.2.220.

Spencer, Keith A. 2019. "The Unsubtle Sexism of the 'Anti-Vax Mom' Meme." *Salon*. 10 February. www.salon.com/2019/02/10/the-unsubtle -sexism-of-the-anti-vax-mom-meme/.

Spigel, Lynn. 2009. *TV by Design: Modern Art and the Rise of Network Television*. Chicago: University of Chicago Press.

Statistics Canada. 2018. "Fertility: Fewer Children, Older Moms." 17 May. https://www150.statcan.gc.ca/n1/pub/11-630-x/11-630-x2014002-eng.htm.

Stein, R.A. 2017. "The Golden Age of Anti-Vaccine Conspiracies." *Germs* 7, no. 4: 168–70. doi:10.18683/germs.2017.1122.

Stern, Alexandra Minna. 2019. "Alt-Right Women and the 'White Baby Challenge.'" *Salon*. 14 July. www.salon.com/2019/07/14/alt-right -handmaidens-and-the-white-baby-challenge/.

Stolberg, Sheryl Gay. 2020. "More Than 200 Republicans Urge Supreme Court to Weigh Overturning Roe v. Wade." 2 January. *New York Times Online*. www.nytimes.com/2020/01/02/us/politics/republicans -abortion-supreme-court.html.

Story, Kaila Adia. 2014. "Living My Material: An Interview with Patricia Hill Collins." In *Patricia Hill Collins: Reconceiving Motherhood*, ed. Kaila Adia Story, 181–91. Bradford, ON: Demeter Press.

Strafford, Amanda, and Lisa Wood. 2017. "Tackling Health Disparities for People Who Are Homeless? Start with Social Determinants." *International Journal of Environmental Research and Public Health* 14, no. 12: 1535. doi: 10.3390/ijerph14121535.

Straub, Peter. 2002. "Introduction to the Perennial Edition." In Ira Levin, *The Stepford Wives*, vii–xiii. New York: William Morrow.

Sturken, M., and Cartwright, L. 2009. *Practices of Looking: An Introduction to Visual Culture*. Oxford: Oxford University Press.

Sultana, Anjum, and Carmina Ravanera. 2020. *A Feminist Economic Recovery Plan for Canada: Making the Economy Work for Everyone*. Institute for Gender and the Economy (GATE) and YWCA Canada. www.gendereconomy.org/wp-content/uploads/2022/05/Feminist EconomyRecoveryPlanforCanada.pdf.

Swain, John, and Sally French. 2000. "Towards an Affirmation Model of Disability." *Disability and Society* 15, no. 4: 569–82.

Taylor, Keeanga-Yamahtta. 2016. *From #BlackLivesMatter to Black Liberation*. Chicago: Haymarket Books.

Taylor, Keeanga-Yamahtta. 2017. *How We Get Free: Black Feminism and the Combahee River Collective*. Chicago: Haymarket Books.

Third World Women's Alliance. (1971) 2016. "Women in the Struggle." In *Revolutionary Feminism: Communist Interventions,* 3: 252–5. New York: Communist Research Cluster. https://communistresearchcluster.files.wordpress.com/2016/04/crc_ci_vol_three_2_01.pdf.

Thomas, Melvin, Loren Henderson, and Hayward Derrick Horton, eds. 2022. *Race, Ethnicity, and the COVID-19 Pandemic*. Cincinnati: University of Cincinnati Press.

Thurer, S. 1995. *The Myths of Motherhood: How Culture Reinvents the Good Mother*. Harmondsworth, UK: Penguin.

Tillson, Patricia Ann. 1996. "The Defeat of the Equal Rights Amendment: A Propaganda Analysis of Phillis Schlafly's STOP ERA Campaign." Master's thesis, University of Houston.

Today. 2018. "Fixer Upper Star Joanna Gaines Gives a Tour of Her Family Farmhouse." *Today*, YouTube. 6 November. www.youtube.com/watch?v=W8rKww2nxgI.

Tolley, K. 2019. "School Vaccination Wars: The Rise of Anti-Science in the American Anti-Vaccination Societies, 1879–1929." *History of Education Quarterly* 59, no. 2: 161–94. doi:10.1017/heq.2019.3.

Tong, Rosemarie. 2007. "Gender-Based Disparities East/West: Rethinking the Burden of Care in the United States and Taiwan." *Bioethics* 21, no. 9: 488–99.

Totenberg, Nina, and Sarah McCammon. 2022. "Supreme Court Overturns Roe v. Wade, Ending Right to Abortion Upheld for Decades." NPR. 24 June. www.npr.org/2022/06/24/1102305878/supreme-court-abortion -roe-v-wade-decision-overturn.

Toupin, Louise. 2018. *Wages for Housework: A History of an International Feminist Movement, 1972–1977*. Translated by Kathe Roth. Vancouver: UBC Press.

Towns, Armond. 2022. "Transporting Blackness: Black Materialist Media Theory." In *Re-Understanding Media: Feminist Extensions of Marshall McLuhan*, ed, Sarah Sharma and Rianka Singh, 23–35. Durham, NC: Duke University Press.

Truth and Reconciliation Commission of Canada. 2015. *Honouring the Truth, Reconciling the Future: Summary of the Final Report of the Truth and Reconciliation Commission of Canada*. https://ehprnh2mwo3.exactdn .com/wp-content/uploads/2021/01/Executive_Summary_English _Web.pdf.

Tuck, Eve, and K. Wayne Yang. 2012. "Decolonization Is Not a Metaphor." *Decolonization: Indigeneity, Education and Society* 1, no. 1: 1–40.

Tufekci, Z. 2013. "'Not This One': Social Movements, the Attention Economy, and Microcelebrity Networked Action." *American Behavioral Scientist* 57, no. 7: 848–70. https://doi.org/10.1177/0002764213479369.

Ussher, Jane M. 2006. *Managing the Monstrous Feminine: Regulating the Reproductive Body*. London: Routledge.

Vandenbeld Giles, Melinda, ed. 2014a. *Mothering in the Age of Neoliberalism*. Bradford, ON: Demeter Press.

Vandenbeld Giles, Melinda. 2014b. "Mothers of the World Unite: Gender Inequality and Poverty under the Neo-liberal State." *Development* 57, nos 3–4: 416–22.

Vandenbeld Giles, Melinda. 2020. "From Home to House: Neoliberalism, Mothering, and the De-domestication of the Private Sphere?" In *The Routledge Companion to Motherhood*, ed. Lynn O'Brien Hallstein, Andrea O'Reilly, and Melinda Vandenbeld Giles. London: Routledge.

Vogel, Lise. (1983) 2013. *Marxism and the Oppression of Women: Toward a Unitary Theory*. Boston: Brill.

Wagman, Ira. 2002. "Wheat, Barley, Hops, and Citizenship." *Velvet Light Trap* 50: 77–89.

Walker, Rebecca. 1992. "Becoming the Third Wave." *Ms. Magazine*. January, 39–41.

Waring, Marilyn. 1988. *If Women Counted: A New Feminist Economics*. New York: HarperCollins.

Waters, Mark, dir. 2004. *Mean Girls*. Paramount Pictures.

Watling, E. 2019. "The 200-Year History of the Anti-Vaxxer Movement: From 'Cowpox Face' to Autism Claims." *Newsweek*. 3 March. www.newsweek.com/history-anti-vaxxers-vaccination-1358403.

Watson, Amanda D. 2020. *The Juggling Mother: Coming Undone in the Age of Anxiety*. Vancouver: UBC Press.

Weaver, Jackson. 2022. "Why Encanto's 'We Don't Talk about Bruno' Is Dominating Charts." *CBC News*. 5 February. www.cbc.ca/news/entertainment/encanto-music-popularity-1.6340471.

Weber, Max. (1905) 2001. *The Protestant Ethic and the Spirit of Capitalism*. Translated by Talcott Parsons. London: Routledge.

Weisholtz, Drew. 2021. "Chip and Joanna Gaines Respond to Claims of Racism, Anti-LGBTQ Bias." *Today*. 1 July. www.today.com/popculture/chip-joanna-gaines-respond-claims-racism-anti-lgbtq-bias-t224251.

The What / Rug Doctor Woman Ad. 2017. *Know Your Meme*. https://knowyourmeme.com/memes/the-what-rug-doctor-woman-ad.

Wiggins, B.W. 2019. *The Discursive Power of Memes in Digital Culture: Ideology, Semiotics, and Intertextuality*. London: Routledge.

Williams, A. 2020. "Black Memes Matter: #LivingWhileBlack with Becky and Karen," *Social Media + Society* 6, no. 4. https://doi.org/10.1177/2056305120981047.

Williams, Raymond. 1974. *Television: Technology and Cultural Form*. London: Routledge.

Wilson, Julie A., and Emily Chivers Yochim. 2017. *Mothering through Precarity: Women's Work and Digital Media*. Durham, NC: Duke University Press.

Wong, Julia Carrie. 2019a. "Anti-vaxx Propaganda Has Gone Viral on Facebook. Pinterest Has a Cure." *Guardian*. 21 February. www.theguardian.com/technology/2019/feb/20/pinterest-anti-vaxx-propaganda-search-facebook.

Wong, Julia Carrie. 2019b. "Facebook to Ban Anti-vaxx Ads in New Push against 'Vaccine Hoaxes.'" *Guardian*. 7 March. www.theguardian.com/technology/2019/mar/07/facebook-anti-vaxx-vaccine-hoax-ads.

Woolf, Virginia. 1937. "Professions for Women." A speech delivered to the National Society for Women's Service. www.wheelersburg.net/Downloads/Woolf.pdf.

World Health Organization. 2019. *Ten Threats to Global Health in 2019*. www.who.int/emergencies/ten-threats-to-global-health-in-2019.

Wylie, Phillip. (1943) 1996. *Generation of Vipers*. Funks Grove, IL: Dalkey Archive Press.

Wynter, Sylvia. 2000. "Beyond Miranda's Meanings: Un/Silencing the 'Demonic Ground' of Caliban's 'Woman.'" In *The Black Feminist Reader*, ed. Joy James and T. Denean Sharpley-Whiting, 109–30. Hoboken: Blackwell.

Wynter, Sylvia. 2006. "On How We Mistook the Map for the Territory, and Re-Imprisoned Ourselves in Our Unbearable Wrongness of Being, of Desetre." In *Not Only the Master's Tools: African-American Studies in Theory and Practice*, ed. Lewis R. Gordon and Jane Anna Gordon, 107–72. Boulder, CO: Paradigm Publishers.

Yergeau, M. 2018. *Authoring Autism: On Rhetoric and Neurological Queerness*. Durham, NC: Duke University Press.

Young, Iris Marion. 1980. "Socialist Feminism and the Limits of Dual Systems Theory." *Socialist Review* 50, no. 1: 169–88.

Zakaria, Rafia. 2021. *Against White Feminism*. New York: W.W. Norton.

Zhan, Jennifer. 2022. "Chip and Joanna Gaines's Magnolia Network Is Moving to a New Home." *Vulture*. 4 August.

Zochios, Stamatios. 2011. "Lamia: A Sorceress, a Fairy or a Revenant?" *Caietele Echinox* 21: 20–31.

Television Episodes Cited

Chapter 3

Matsumoto, Michael, exec. producer. 2013. "Looking Old But Feeling New." *Fixer Upper*. Season 1, episode 1. High Noon Entertainment.

Matsumoto, Michael, exec. producer. 2014a. "Embracing Revitalization." *Fixer Upper*. Season 1, episode 2. High Noon Entertainment.

Matsumoto, Michael, exec. producer. 2014b. "French Country in Waco." *Fixer Upper*. Season 1, episode 5. High Noon Entertainment.

Matsumoto, Michael, exec. producer. 2014c. "Family Craves Urban Feel." *Fixer Upper*. Season 1, episode 6. High Noon Entertainment.

Matsumoto, Michael, exec. producer. 2014d. "Missionaries' Retreat in Waco." *Fixer Upper*. Season 1, episode 9. High Noon Entertainment.

Matsumoto, Michael, exec. producer. 2015. "Taking a Chance." *Fixer Upper*. Season 2, episode 2. High Noon Entertainment.

Matsumoto, Michael, exec. producer. 2017. "Family Seeks Spacious Upgrade." *Fixer Upper*. Season 5, episode 2. High Noon Entertainment.

Simard, Marc., dir. 2020. "Michael and Elizabeth." *Making It Home with Kortney and Dave*. Season 1, episode 1. Scott Brothers Entertainment, Canada.

Wilkes, James, dir. 2015a. "Who Paints Brick?" *Masters of Flip*. Season 1, episode 1. Rhino Productions, Canada.

Wilkes, James, dir. 2015b. "Don't Be a Hero." *Masters of Flip*. Season 1, episode 9. Rhino Productions, Canada.

Wilkes, James, dir. 2015c. "Tight for Time." *Looking Old but Feeling New*. Season 1, episode 12. Rhino Productions, Canada.

Wilkes, James, dir. 2016. "Classic Charm." *Masters of Flip*. Season 2, episode 10. Rhino Productions, Canada.

Zalameda, Cheryl, dir. 2021. "Joven and Sylvia." *Making It Home with Kortney and Kenny*. Season 2, episode 2. Scott Brothers Entertainment, Canada.

Chapter 5

Modern Family

Chandrasekaran, Vali. 2018. "Good Grief," dir. Beth McCarthy-Miller. Season 10, episode 5 (24 October). Lloyd-Levitan Productions.

Ko, Elaine. 2011. "Princess Party," dir. Michael Spiller. Season 2, episode 15 (16 February). Lloyd-Levitan Productions.

Levitan, Steven. 2009. "The Incident," dir. Jason Winer. Season 1, episode 4 (14 October). Lloyd-Levitan Productions.

Levitan, Steven, Christopher Lloyd, and Abraham Higginbotham. 2017. "Sarge and Pea," dir. James R. Bagdonas. Season 8, episode 11 (11 January). Lloyd-Levitan Productions.

Lloyd, Christopher, Steven Levitan, and Ryan Walls. 2020. "Trees a Crowd," dir. Julie Bowen. Season 11, episode 8 (6 March). Lloyd-Levitan Productions.

Pollock, John, and Ryan Walls. 2016. "Crazy Train," dir. Jim Hensz. Season 7, episode 21 (11 May). Lloyd-Levitan Productions.

Walls, Ryan. 2018. "On the Same Paige," dir. Ryan Case. Season 10, episode 6 (31 October). Lloyd-Levitan Productions.

Zucker, Danny, and Christopher Lloyd. 2013. "Party Crasher," dir. Fred Savage. Season 4, episode 12 (16 January). Lloyd-Levitan Productions.

Shameless

Abbott, Paul. 2011. "We're Going to the Moon," dir. Johnny Campbell. Season 1, episode 2 (30 June). John Wells Production.

Abbott, Paul, and John Wells. 2011. Pilot, dir. Mark Mylod. Season 1, episode 1 (9 January). John Wells Production.

Abbott, Paul, and John Wells. 2013a. "El Gran Canon," dir. John Wells. Season 3, episode 1 (13 January). John Wells Production.

Abbott, Paul, and John Wells. 2013b. "Cascading Failures," dir. Anthony Hemingway. Season 3, episode 6 (24 February). John Wells Production.

Abbott, Paul, and John Wells. 2013c. "A Long Way from Home," dir. Mimi Leder. Season 3, episode 7 (3 March). John Wells Production.

Borstein, Alex. 2012. "Hurricane Monica," dir. Alex Graves. Season 2, episode 9 (11 March). John Wells Production.

Caponera, Cindy. 2011. "Nanna Gallagher Had an Affair," dir. Adam Bernstein. Season 1, episode 10 (13 March). John Wells Production.

Frankel, Etan. 2012. "A Great Cause," dir. Mimi Leader. Season 2, episode 10 (18 March). John Wells Production.

Morgan, LaToya, and Nancy M. Pimental. 2012. "Just Like the Pilgrims Intendent," dir. Mark Mylod. Season 2, episode 11 (25 March). John Wells Production.

O'Malley, Mike. 2012. "Parenthood," dir. Daisy von Scherler Mayer. Season 2, episode 8 (4 March). John Wells Production.

Wells, John. 2012. "Fiona Interrupted," dir. John Wells. Season 2, episode 12 (1 April). John Wells Production.

Wells, John. 2016a. "Ouroboros," dir. Christopher Chulack. Season 7, episode 9 (27 November). John Wells Production.

Wells, John. 2016b. "Ride or Die," dir. Zetna Fuentes. Season 7, episode 10 (4 December). John Wells Production.

Wells, John. 2016c. "Happily Ever After," dir. John M. Valerio. Season 7, episode (11 December). John Wells Production.

Chapter 6

Raised by Wolves

Gabassi, Alex, dir. 2020. "Mass." Season 1, episode 8. London: Scott Free Production Company.

Hawes, James, dir. 2020. "Umbilical." Season 1, episode 9. London: Scott Free Production Company.

Mimica-Gezzan, Sergio, dir. 2020a. "Infected Memory." Season 1, episode 5. London: Scott Free Production Company.

Mimica-Gezzan, Sergio, dir. 2020b. "Lost Paradise." Season 1, episode 6. London: Scott Free Production Company.

Scott, Luke, dir. 2020a. "Virtual Faith." Season 1, episode 3. London: Scott Free Production Company.

Scott, Luke, dir. 2020b. "Nature's Course." Season 1, episode 4. London: Scott Free Production Company.

Scott, Luke, dir. 2020c. "The Beginning." Season 1, episode 10. London: Scott Free Production Company.

Scott, Ridley, dir. 2020a. "Raised by Wolves." Season 1, episode 1. London: Scott Free Production Company.

Scott, Ridley, dir. 2020b. "Pentagram." Season 1, episode 2. London: Scott Free Production Company.

Small, Steve. 2020. Tile sequence. London: Studio AKA.

Index